# THE SHOCK OF HOLINESS

MICHAEL PAKALUK

# The Shock of Holiness

## Finding the Romance of Everyday Life

IGNATIUS PRESS    SAN FRANCISCO

Cover collage:
Digital scans of illuminated manuscripts from the New York Public Library (Spencer Collection MS 6 and *Taccuinum Sanitatis*), the Metropolitan Museum of Art (*The Cloisters Apocalypse*), the Getty Museum (MS 14), and the British Library (*Golf Book of Hours*)

Cover design by Paweł Cetlinski and Thomas Jacobi

To Sarah Esther


Lord, thou only art our King; help me,
who am alone and have no helper but thee.
—Esther 14:3

# CONTENTS

## Part V: Life and Manners

# PREFACE

These essays are written within a household of faith, and, for those outside the household, they are invitations to enter and join the life within. I might have called them "Essays in Re-enchantment". The recovery of wonder and re-enchantment, which many of my contemporaries look for, is at bottom a recovery of childhood. And yet only in the household of Christian faith is childhood preserved or, if lost, recovered. Enchantment is one of those things that can be acquired only as a side effect of seeking something else. Seek it on its own, and you will get entangled in traps and fantasies. Seek the truth about God and human nature, and you may just find that you have rediscovered your childhood, wonder, and enchantment along the way.

A word of warning is in order. These essays are by design compact and concise. Not infrequently they need to be read with something like the care with which one reads poetry or solves a crossword. Often, they must be "taken slowly" or be "picked apart". I do not want to waste your time by saying in many words what could be said in few. I do want to entertain you by conveying subtle thoughts quickly and with indirection. These essays are designed to challenge, perplex, and in that way delight you. I want to say new things and to say them well.

Almost all of these essays first appeared online in a daily magazine, *The Catholic Thing*. You can still find and read them at the magazine's website. So then, why make a book out of them? Because the online archive is actually difficult to discover. Because, in any case, going to an online archive and reading through past essays is not something we do. Because it is one thing to read a single brief essay with the morning email, which is good, and another thing altogether to sit for hours at a computer, or on the internet with a device, when holding a printed book in your hands would be much better. Also, I have edited these essays, picking out the best of them for you and placing them in groups and in order. This is itself good, but also, when they are so arranged, deeper views and connections become clear. Also, it is not so easy to recommend an online archive to friends, and especially to young people, while it is easy to buy a book and give it to someone. Besides, these essays (it is the premise of this book) have a value beyond the ephemeral and by rights should be placed in a medium where they can make a claim side-by-side with other books. I might just say: it is the time-honored practice of essayists to do what I am doing here.

An essay does not need to be long to make a lasting point. Even today I still draw upon the lessons I learned from brief essays by C.S. Lewis that I encountered as a college student, such as "Meditation in a Tool Shed" and "First and Second Things". My hope is that in helping similarly some college student or other reader today, I can repay in part a debt of gratitude I owe to Lewis, Chesterton, Father James Schall, and other great Christian essayists.

In graduate school while reading the *Summa contra Gentiles* of Saint Thomas Aquinas, I encountered a confession of Saint Hilary of Poitiers that expressed what I myself thought. Although each thing that we do is an implicit word, the words here are explicit and published.

> I am aware that I owe this to God as the chief duty of my
> life, that my every word and sense may speak of Him.
> —*De Trinitate* 1, 37[1]

---

[1] Quoted in Thomas Aquinas, *On the Truth of the Catholic Faith: Summa contra Gentiles*, trans. Anton C. Pegis (New York: Image Books, 1955), bk. 1, chap. 2, p. 62.

Part I

# The Romance of Daily Life

I

# Moms at Mass, and Other Heroes

Like other professional men, if I want to attend weekday Mass, I have a choice between an early Mass in my parish and a midday Mass near my work. I love seeing colleagues at the later Mass and the thrill of the sacrifice that comes specifically from putting work aside for the moment and giving that time directly to God. But at the morning Mass, I have the great blessing of being instructed in Christian wisdom by the moms there with little children.

My parish is Saint Jerome's in Hyattsville, celebrated as a strong community in a "Benedict option" sort of way. Many families live within walking distance of the church. On any weekday, there can be ten or fifteen moms at Mass. Most have one child with them, but some bring two or three—perhaps one in a sling, another in a stroller, and a third getting around on his own steam. If the family is homeschooling, sometimes older children, too, get up early and lend a hand.

At most parishes, there will be a couple of moms like this, not always the same ones at every Mass. In a city, where there are many parishes and people improvise to catch the most convenient Mass, these moms with children will come to know one another, forming a kind of secret conspiracy of real Catholic devotion.

I mentioned being schooled in Christian wisdom, first of all—paradoxically—by the example of the husband and father, who is not there. These moms are mainly home-makers, although some, of course, will have jobs on the side. The point is that the husband has not insisted that they go out into the workforce full time, as many do. He is willing to accept the cares and occasionally large sacri-fices that go along with raising a family on a single income. That is, he is a highly noble figure in our day. The mom and the father together testify to the priority of their chil-dren over wealth and security.

Secondly, I am instructed by the heroism of the mom. It is important to emphasize that it is heroism, "above and beyond the call of duty". (More, shortly, on "duty".) How heroic? Morning Mass is a deeply ordered act, which the mom manages to set up at the start of the day, at a time of life that inherently resists order. Her presence at that ser-vice has all the character of a beachhead on Iwo Jima; the Consecration and her Communion, a raising of the flag over Mount Suribachi.

To get there at all, she has wrestled a child to change a diaper and wrestled with a couple of others, too, or pleaded and cajoled, to get them dressed. In winter, there are layers of clothing, potentially depressing to put on, knowing that they have to come off and be put away in an hour. Always there is the principle of household entropy at work, the tendency to disorder.

Her path goes all uphill. The church will be cold in the winter and hot in the summer. Most likely the homily will be uninspiring: she is grateful if it does not knock her back ("women do not have to breed like rabbits") or promote a heresy, like the one she was arguing against with a Prot-estant friend at a book club last week. Do not discount the small mortification of often appearing in public not "put

together". (In that sense she did give up the heels and lip-
stick, as some pro-abortion ads warn.)

But above all there is the repeated mortification involving the "main show", the reason she is there at all, to pray
and worship. Her children are fussy or asking her for things.
They cannot sit still and run all over. She has to take them
to the back, yet again. She sits on a chair in the vestibule,
plays give-and-take with her toddler, and can barely hear
anything in the sanctuary. It is far from the romantic ideal
of peaceful communion with God. *What is the point of this?*
It is not even clear she is improving in anything, she thinks.

But her perseverance proves important truths, to which
over time she becomes a "martyr" or witness. Others may
read about them in books, but she at least learns them by
concrete experience. *Consolations in prayer do not matter.*
*We give ourselves to God through the will, not the imagination.*
*Grace will assuredly be imparted by the objective character of the*
*sacrament and a believer's subjective willingness to receive.*

In simply getting to "the place of grace" in the morning,
she is standing beside the Cross with Mary and becomes,
like her, a "spiritual vessel, vessel of honor". She cannot
"feel" the grace that she gains at the Mass and that flows
out from her to her family, relatives, friends, and prayer
intentions, but as an exercise of faith she trusts that it is so.

We live in a society where people are afraid to praise
anyone (but in personal life only) for fear of seeming by
implication to criticize everyone else. I know that. Let's be
plain then: there are many moms who want to get to weekday Mass but cannot manage it, or who started and could
not continue. Likewise, there are couples where the mom
would love to stay at home and cannot, or where, in conscience before God, they believe that she can but should
work full time outside the home nonetheless. I am not criticizing these brethren in the slightest, not by a long shot.

I say, instead, for Christians the strange "logic" of a parable seems at play. Remember the workers who were hired at the last moment but got the same payment as those who bore the brunt of the day's work? Yes, there are degrees of glory, but that parable would seem to hold for more than differences in time. Who knows how the Lord will repay in His generosity? But that moms at Mass are heroes of the faith, among others not at Mass, that is a sure thing.

2

# In Praise of Holy Water

It used to be said that the priest "made" holy water; he did not simply bless it. The rite is still in the Roman ritual. The priest makes holy water by adding exorcized salt to exorcized water. He adds salt in imitation of the prophet Elisha, who thus purified the waters of Jericho (2 Kings 2:21): "Thus says the LORD, I have made this water wholesome; henceforth neither death nor miscarriage shall come from it."

Holy water, in this rite, is understood as a pure creature directly conveying the power of God. Hence, both salt and water must first be exorcized, on the grounds that the Fall reverberated throughout all of material creation, giving Satan a dominion even over lifeless elements.

The exorcisms are bracing. For example, of the salt:

Our help is in the name of the Lord, Who hath made heaven and earth. I exorcise thee, thou creature salt, by the living God, by the true God, by the holy God ... that thou may become health of soul and body to all who take thee; that every delusion and wickedness and snare of diabolical cunning and every unclean spirit may depart from the place in which thou shalt be sprinkled, when adjured by Him who is to come to judge the living and the dead and the world by fire. Amen.

An exorcism is not simply a prayer but, as the philosopher J. L. Austin would say, "something done with words".[1] It remakes the salt and water, turning them in a special way into instruments against the Evil One. Thus, the priest's final prayer over the mixture entreats God to sanctify it so that "wheresoever it shall be sprinkled, by the invocation of Thy holy name, all troubling of unclean spirits may be cast out, and the dread of the poisonous servant be chased far away."

The holy water in churches today, I believe, is typically blessed, not made, the priest saying a prayer of blessing and making a sign of the cross over it, often in the context of Mass. Far be it from me, not a liturgist, to claim that even holy water has been watered down. Yes, of course, I too have the thought, "If we *could* follow the example of a great prophet, and if we *could* use exorcized matter—why in the world *would* we *not* avail ourselves of these additional helps?"

Surely not on the minimalist grounds that the grace of Christ is sufficient, because then the argument for having holy water at all would be taken away. Moreover, this Christ is a mediator, after all, who in His life on earth showed a strong liking for working through mediating matter, such as spittle and dirt.

Rather, from experience I know that blessed water works very effectively against the devil.

I mean first of all "experience" in the broad and proper sense, of *what has been experienced by those we trust*—not in the attenuated Cartesian sense of *what has impinged upon my own senses in particular*. In this sense, Saint Teresa of Avila's

---

[1] J. L. Austin (John Langshaw), Marina Sbisa, and J. O. Urmson, *How to Do Things with Words*, 2nd ed., ed. J. O. Urmson and Marina Sbisa (Cambridge, Mass.: Harvard Univ. Press, 1975).

experience is mine, too: "I know by frequent experience that there is nothing which puts the devils to flight like holy water."[2]

Many friends have told me the same thing. They were troubled at night by twisted dreams, for instance—and after they began sprinkling holy water on the bed each night and said a Hail Mary or three, the problem vanished and never returned. Something my own life experiences tend to corroborate.

Many of the friends I have mentioned, naturally enough, do not omit holy water when tucking in their children. But this leads to another reason for praising it, beyond its utility, namely, how attractive it is to children and child-like adults.

As children we marvel at bells, smoke, fire. The Church is right to appeal to our senses in this way. But consider that water, like fire, is not "supposed" to be within buildings. So even a small votive candle—that little point of brilliant fire, guarded by the wax but dangerous if it were to break out—can signify something transcendent, prayer ascending to God and light descending.

For a similar reason, we lean forward to get sprinkled with Holy Water on Easter Sunday, and we like to dip our fingers in the holy water font. As the water is not where it is "supposed" to be, it easily signifies inflowing grace from God, while it should lead us to consider our own Baptism and the purifying efficacy of sacramental Confession.

The family is a domestic church, not on its own, but as participating in the life of the Church. That little bottle of holy water in the household, then, testifies to the

---

[2] Saint Teresa of Avila, *The Life of St. Teresa of Jesus of the Order of Our Lady of Carmel*, trans. David Lewis, with additional notes and introduction by Rev. Benedict Zimmerman, O.C.D. (London: T. Baker, 1904), chap. 31, 4, p. 253.

reality of Holy Orders and the power of the Church in the sacraments.

As holy water is held to be precious, and it comes solely from the priest, the priesthood is honored by it. As we get holy water freely—we need only bring a bottle to the church and fill it—it teaches that the most precious things in life have no price. They are freely given by God, if we simply look for them in the right place.

Finally, as water is an element, and holy water is a blessed element, it testifies to the goodness of creation, to how grace completes nature, and to the logic of the Incarnation.

There is a catechism contained in holy water. Alternatively, we can say that the true Church would, of course, have devised it. Alternatively, as truth is overdetermined by evidence, we can also say that the existence and use of holy water, like forty other things, are almost on their own a reason to become a Catholic.

Following Saint Francis, I want to say, "Praised be You, my Lord, through Sister *Holy* Water, which is very useful and humble and precious and chaste."

# 3

# The Lord of Substance

How precisely might someone go about showing that he had authority, mastery, and power over substances? Bear with me: this is an important question.

It is a curious fact about the human imagination that we are slow to extend miraculous power indefinitely. Someone who, for instance, had the power to cure a leper instantaneously, logically also has the power to restore sight to the blind instantaneously. The reason is that any miracle involves causing something to begin to exist from nothing, which implies infinite power. And infinite power can be applied for any effect whatsoever.

But demonstrably those who first followed Jesus, after He had cured a leper, needed to be shown that He could give sight to the blind—and make the lame walk, the dumb speak, and the deaf hear. After He had raised Jairus' daughter, the raising of Lazarus should have been obviously implied, but apparently it was not.

Hence my question about substances. Suppose someone with infinite power wanted to demonstrate to us poor human beings, with such limited imaginations, that he had power, too, over substances: How would he do it?

By "power over substances", I do not mean the power to change (grant: instantaneously) the position or quality or arrangement of substances. There are lots of X-rays in

Lourdes of pilgrims who arrived with a misshapen hip or other structure that was restored instantaneously after a bath in the waters there. That is not the kind of thing I mean, which is, rather, the power to change one substance into another substance. A philosopher would say: a power over substances *qua* substances, like the power that the alchemists sought to change lead into gold.

Let's complicate the question and ask: Suppose someone with infinite power wanted to demonstrate to us that he had the power to change a substance while preserving the appearance of the original substance—say, change lead into gold, while it continues to look like lead. How could he do so?

I have always wondered why walking on water impressed the disciples so much, as it clearly did. Is it not simply a form of suspension? Imagine someone hanging from invisible cords and held up so that he does not sink. But that is not actually the impression that walking on water makes. It is rather that something that, of its nature, is supposed to be unstable and liquid behaves as a solid, while still looking for all that like a liquid.

That is the power displayed: turning liquid stuff into, somehow, for this person in his circumstances, a solid. Not all of it, but surely some of it. And yet not in its appearance, since it still looks like water. The only thing that changes is its "substance".

A substance is literally what underlies, what "stands under". What stood under Our Lord, I think, when He walked on water was not water, although it looked like water.

The Gospels that recount the walking on water (Mt 14:22–33, Mk 6:45–52, Jn 6:16–21) all take pains to say that this happened immediately after the feeding of the five thousand. "Immediately afterward He compelled the disciples to get into the boat and to go ahead of Him to the other side", Matthew says. Mark echoes the same, and John. The walking on water, surely, is a deliberately crafted miracle; there was no other reason why the Lord did not get into the boat with them, except to display this power. But why did He do it just then? He Himself linked the feeding with the walking. Why?

He walked "on the sea" and "on the water", Matthew says (Mt 14:26, 28). There were four main substances according to the thought of the ancient world: earth, water, air, and fire. It is not possible to walk miraculously on air or fire, only water. To demonstrate power over substance, through walking upon a substance, would be possible only for water.

The old translations render the Lord's Prayer as "give us this day our supersubstantial bread", that is, bread that is "upon the substance". Saint Jerome's Vulgate renders it thus in Latin, and also the original Douay-Rheims in English (1610). The King James Bible (1611) with its "daily bread" in contrast seems to have influenced English speakers at least.

The underlying Greek word, *epiousios*, attested by all the authoritative manuscripts, is used in only two places in all extant Greek texts: in Matthew's version of the Lord's Prayer and in Luke's. It is used nowhere else. Not in the Septuagint; not in any philosopher; not in orators; not in literature. Origen (circa A.D. 185–253) knew nothing of the word in ordinary Greek and speculated that it was coined by the Evangelists. If that was the case, surely, they did so in consultation with the Lord. The word's most obvious etymology is *epi-*, "upon", *ousia*, "substance". No other proposed etymology quite makes sense.

Most importantly, there are several ways of saying "daily" in Greek. Why would the Evangelists concoct a new word if all they wanted to say about the bread was something mundane, that it was given or provided "daily"? Why use a novel word for this idea—a word that, in its most natural meaning, says something rather different, "upon the substance"?

On the other hand, suppose that the Lord wanted to convey that the feeding of the five thousand was only a type. Suppose He wanted to convey, in a mystical way, and as a foreshadowing, the idea of what we call "transubstantiation"—namely, that in the Eucharist, the bread changes in its substance while its appearance stays the same. Would it not make sense that He would deliberately link together, with that feeding, some kind of display— the best display, maybe the only possible display—that He had the power to change one substance into another while keeping its appearance the same?

The disciples when they see Him shout, "It is a phantasm!", an appearance (Mt 14:26; author's translation, hereafter abbreviated AT). He replies: "I am." He might just as well have said: "This is my body."

# 4

# Do This in Remembrance of Me

"This is my body which is given for you. Do this in remembrance of me" (Lk 22:19). Thus, a rather wooden and literal translation, which preserves the word order and the oddities of the original language, clearly connoting something strange and mysterious. What does it mean?

When I was a Protestant, I would hear that the Eucharist is solely a memorial, no different from the Washing of Feet or Stations of the Cross, because Jesus had said so: it was "in remembrance".

Of course, it does not follow. A remembrance need not be solely a remembrance, and the very thing remembered, or something close to it, can be the means of remembrance. For instance, it makes perfect sense for a married couple to regard their intimate union as a remembrance of their wedding, their original act of union. But need it be said that an act that can procreate a child is hardly a "mere" remembrance?

I have wondered about the origin of this modern Protestant argument, based on the words "do this in remembrance of me." The Fathers and the Scholastics, from my study, seem not to have been concerned about it. Apparently, they did not see the threat of false argument here. I think there are two reasons for this.

The first is that they were keenly attuned to how pronouns that point—like "this" and "me"—were at work in the Last Supper.

For example, Aquinas raises an interesting problem,[1] which goes as follows: The word of God can of course effect what it signifies. Therefore, we grant that Jesus' statement "This is my body", through its being uttered, can make it so that the bread has become His body. When Jesus begins to say that statement, however, the word "this" refers to the bread, which has not yet been made His body. Therefore, "This is my body" would mean "This bread is my body", which would be a false statement. But Jesus is not saying anything false.

Aquinas resolves the problem by emphasizing that Jesus did not say, after all, "this bread", but rather simply "this", which in the context must mean "that which underlies and is hidden here by the appearances that you see and touch." At the start of the statement, "This is my body", he holds, nothing else is picked up and referred to, and, by the end, that which underlies and is hidden is indeed His body. So the statement is never false, and it becomes true precisely in effecting what it signified.

You can see that Fathers and Doctors who thought deeply in this way, when they next came to "this in remembrance of me", took "this" to point to exactly what had just been done. And if what had just been done had turned bread into the Lord's body, then, obviously, "this", which we do today, does so as well.

The second reason the Scholastics did not even suspect that the "mere remembrance" view could be true is that, attuned as they were to the importance of "this", they would have seen instantly the similar importance of "me".

[1] Thomas Aquinas, *Summa Theologica* III, q. 78, art. 6.

Here we should step back and understand that the Greek word rendered "remembrance" (*anamnēsis*) means, strictly, being prompted to perceive again someone or something you had perceived before, through some present likeness or some association. Importantly, what you are prompted to perceive again may exist in the present; it is only your own prior acquaintance that is in the past.

An example that I take from Plato (*Phaedo*, 74), makes this clear. Suppose Simmias and Cebes are such close friends that they are never seen apart. You are acquainted with both. You come home one day and see Cebes in your house. Immediately you think or "perceive" that Simmias is in your house also. And when he comes in from another room, it is true to say that Cebes, through his presence, led you to perceive Simmias there, too.

You can see how misleading it is to call such a process a "remembrance". Still, it, or perhaps "recollection", is probably the best English word for it. Strictly, it is a matter of being prompted by a likeness or association to perceive someone or something of your acquaintance yet again. (Latin, *commemoratio*, is closer to the Greek than the English equivalents.)

You can see, then, that the Fathers who understood the Greek would in no way be tempted to believe that, because the act was "for an *anamnēsis*", Jesus was not truly present in the act. Rather, Our Lord's language of "me" suggested the opposite. He did not say "do this in remembrance of my life" or "of my sacrifice" or "of my teachings that you will read about later in gospels". After all, He was there, presiding over "this", which He commanded them all to repeat regularly, In that setting, "me" would suggest that through "this" they would perceive *Him* again, not a memory of Him.

If this truth is not what is so cleverly taught by Our Lord's appearance after the Resurrection on the road to

Emmaus, then I do not know what is. Surely it is not a coincidence that this episode is found in the only Gospel, Luke's, that includes the language about remembrance.

Some men are walking along the road who had perceived the Lord previously in Jerusalem. Our Lord shows up, but "the eyes" of the men, Luke says, are kept from recognizing Him (24:16). That is, only the visible appearance is different, not what underlies.

If Our Lord had not deliberately stopped them from recognizing Him, then they would have simply seen Him directly, that is, there would have been no space for *anamnēsis*, for "remembrance", to enter in. As it is, already encountering Him in disguise, their "hearts are burning within them". So they *do* perceive Him! Although they do not understand it yet.

But then, "when he was at table with them, he took the bread and blessed and broke it, and gave it to them"—very nearly the same language as Luke had used for the Last Supper! With that, they perceive once more ... and what they perceive is not a memory from the distant past, but Him, right there, really present with them.

# 5

## *Amor Meus Crucifixus Est*[1]

I want to put before you some thoughts on the meaning of the crucifix. I have in mind the standard crucifix found in a parish church, with a white unblemished corpus, depicting Our Lord still alive, and "INRI" written above. Like all Christians, I love a plain cross of wood, which invites us to embrace it. But the crucifix seems an even superior object of devotion. Can we say why?

There are two traditional reasons. First, the crucifix—more than a plain cross—resembles the serpent on a stake: "As Moses lifted up the serpent in the wilderness, so must the Son of man be lifted up, that whoever believes in him may have eternal life" (Jn 3:14). Why, then, diminish this healing sign? Or how do we "believe in him" if we remove Him? The mere cross in comparison is as if a bare stake, that which lifts up but not the One lifted up.

Second, the crucifix seems to express better the basic Christian message, as explained by Saint Paul: "When I came to you, brethren, I ... decided to know nothing among you except Jesus Christ and him crucified" (1 Cor 2:1–2). Saint Paul says, not that he restricts his preaching to "the cross", but rather to "Christ crucified". These reasons are strong and presumably alone explain why, as exorcists

[1] Latin, "A crucified is my beloved."

say, devils flee especially from the crucifix. But can we add other reasons?

Here is the sort of thing I mean: All of the Apostles, with a notable exception, fled when Our Lord was crucified. Therefore, these official "witnesses of the Lord from the beginning", strangely, failed to witness His main saving act, the very reason why He came into the world. The crucifix, then, captures *for us* what they missed.

But more than that: we know that Saint John and Mary the Mother of Our Lord did keep watch at the foot of the Cross. The crucifix is distinctively the view of Saint John and Mary. So, when you and I contemplate the crucifix today, we take our place alongside them; we see what they alone saw; we enter into solidarity with them and become identified with them.

Another reason is found in the words on the crucifix, "Jesus of Nazareth, king of the Jews" (INRI). Behold the crafty Providence of God, which caused the chief Roman official of that time and place, as if against his intention, to give testimony to the truth about the Lord. Are you not heartened to think: If God could cause even the Roman Empire thus to bend its knee, what can He not do in any age?

Or what about what the standard crucifix *omits*: it does *not* show any signs of a scourging? Saints have told us, as the Shroud of Turin corroborates, that the brutal Roman scourging tore every inch of His flesh, so that His body became bloody, pulpy.

Pious instinct, apparently, while knowing these truths, has judged that they are literally "obscene"—that is, better left off stage. And this I love: the standard crucifix in this manner conveys Our Lord's modesty and delicacy. He does not wish even to give the *appearance* of reproaching us.

Precisely through what is absent, we have scope to make up the difference: we can, if we wish, supply the awful wounds in our imagination. These wounds, caused by our sins, represent them; thus, by adding them freely ourselves, it is as if we confess them.

Here are some other remarkable traits about the crucifix.

First, on the crucifix, the body of the Lord is lifted off the ground and placed in "the air". We—with our scaffolding, elevators, and skyscrapers—do not even notice that this is unusual. Yet the Fathers of the Church were so taken with this aspect—that a crucifixion implied a suspension in air—that they held that the element of "air" (traditionally also a dwelling place of demons) was thereby purified and sanctified, just as Our Lord's Baptism affected all waters.

Second, on the crucifix, Our Lord assumes a posture not seen in ordinary life, namely, standing upright, legs together, with arms outstretched. The posture is so unusual that Leonardo's drawing of it, *Vitruvian Man*, has become iconic. Leonardo was not drawing Christ on the Cross but intending to illustrate the proportions of the human body: a man standing upright with outstretched arms is inscribed perfectly by a square (that is, a man's "wingspan" is generally equal to his height).

For Leonardo, the proportions internal to the human body, a "microcosm", testified to man's ordered place within a universe of law and proportion, the "macrocosm". But the crucifix, through the same bodily form, teaches this very truth at its deepest, spiritual level: "He humbled himself and became obedient unto death, even death on a cross" (Phil 2:8). More than this: because the hands of the Vitruvian man face downward, while Our Lord's face outward, this display of humility on the Cross is clearly, at the same time, a priestly embrace.

Third, the standard crucifix depicts Our Lord as still alive, even though salvation is fully accomplished only at His death ("It is finished", Jn 19:30). But this, too, is remarkable: everyone who has ever kept vigil at a death-bed knows how precious those last hours are; but it seems improper to try to capture them, and we do not do so—perhaps because we recognize intuitively that death for us is a penalty for sin. For Our Lord it is different: since His death was unwarranted but freely accepted, we can depict His "deathbed" always and are invited to keep vigil always.

The crucifix and the cross: the former is found almost solely in churches in which Our Lord is Really Present, which suggests a last recommendation: the crucifix with its substantial corpus is simply a better sign that, indeed, "This is my body" and "This is my blood."

# 6

# Simple, Binding Gifts

I find a common confusion in the use of the phrase "free gift". Someone gives a free gift, properly speaking, if he was not bound to give it. No legal constraint or moral obligation or physical coercion dictated the gift. The giver gave it freely, perhaps because it struck him as good or he felt pity. But people get confused and think that a "free gift" means that the recipient is not bound through receiving it. All gifts bind, however. There is no such thing as a gift with "no strings attached".

The *bindingness* of gifts is attested to in so-called "gift economies", such as the mafia. You simply do not want a "free" gift from a mafioso, as you will eventually be asked to repay, on the mafioso's terms.

Or consider flatterers, who lose their freedom because they do not see how the binding works in their case. They think that by saying what the boss wants to hear, they gain control over the boss, who now has to show them favors. But the boss recognizes that the flatterer only said what was supposed to please him—he never regarded it as a free gift—while he thinks his own indulgence of the obviously craven flatterer *is* a free gift. Thus, in his eyes the flatterer becomes successively more bound, even as the flatterer misguidedly presumes he is getting more and more control.

If I had to place my finger on *the* false idea of our time, the root of all other heresies, it would be that gifts do not bind. Perhaps the idea had its origin long ago in the Protestant assertion of salvation by faith, not works. What that declaration was supposed to mean is that we do not earn our salvation or otherwise obligate God to save us, say, by obedience to the ceremonial law. Salvation is a free gift. God was not constrained to save us. He did so of His own mercy. But it does not follow that once we are saved, if we are, that we are not seriously bound as a result.

I will leave it to you to trace out how "autonomy", our lack of care for the common good, the general expectation of free stuff, our attitudes toward public debt and future generations, the general preference for "spirituality" over "religion" (i.e., being bound)—how these and other bad attitudes flow from this central falsehood.

Of course, if we at least implicitly recognize that gifts do bind, then, to extricate ourselves from bonds and to "cast their cords from us" (Ps 2:3), it becomes necessary to deny that what we have received is a gift. It was the result of chance or necessity.

Christian "universalism", the view that God cannot help but save His rational creatures, that His moral nature requires it, is a vast exercise in denying the reality of the gift of salvation. It thereby sets its adherents free from any obligation to act in response.

All human life is a free gift from God, of course. And that you have this particular life, that you are you, rather than someone else, is also a gift. But one way of construing Christian marriage is that it clarifies and testifies to the gratuitousness. The inherent consequences of a process or state into which we freely enter we also freely will.

A child conceived in a free marriage is given his life by his parents freely because the marriage is free. Therefore, it is more evident and easier to see that he is bound. But

a child conceived in a chance hook-up or some cohab-
itation that was persisted in because it was inconvenient
to separate?

We must conclude that there is a fundamental difference in consciousness between a child conceived within
a free marriage and someone not so conceived. Piety is
easier for the one than the other.

One way to view "as we forgive our debtors" is that
Christianity is intent on making the bindingness of free
gifts even more salient. The Faith emphasizes even more
how someone is bound by being the recipient of a freely
bestowed good, while minimizing how someone becomes
bound by having freely done something bad. It locates the
more serious obligations in the right places.

I am not sure that there is any genuine motive for the
Christian reform of society other than a conviction of being bound because one has been saved. Not enthrallment
with the glorious history of Christendom, not love of
beauty, not awe in the face of sublime nature, not alle-
giance to the pope, not even admiration of the saints.

Converts may look to the before and after of their conversion for clear evidence of their salvation, and Protestant "testimonies" are edifying for doing so. But Catholics
have usually turned to the Passion.

Contemplating the Passion, Saint Alphonsus Liguori
wrote, Therefore, O my Jesus, I cannot any longer, without injustice, dispose of myself, or of my own concerns,
since Thou has made me Thine by purchasing me through
Thy death. My body, my soul, my life are no longer mine;
they are Thine, and entirely Thine. . . . If thou, my God,
art thus become mad, as it were, for the love of me, how is
it that I do not become mad for the love of God?[1]

---

[1] Alphonsus Maria de Liguori, *The Passion and the Death of Jesus Christ*, ed.
Eugene Grimm (Brooklyn: Redemptorist Fathers, 1927), chap. 1, sec. 8, p. 31.

"You are not your own," Saint Paul writes. "You were bought with a price. So glorify God in your body" (1 Cor 6:19–20).

The complete offering up, for God's purposes, of all of your external goods, even the good that is your body and its life, and this done with intense ardor—have these motives not always been the Christian basis of great awakenings and reforms?

"What shall I render to the LORD for all his bounty to me? I will lift up the chalice of salvation and call on the name of the LORD" (Ps 116:12–13). And the Eucharist has always been the burning fire that inflames such ardor.

# 7

# How to Repay the Love of Christ

The most fundamental problem that confronts a Christian, in my view, is how to *answer to* the Passion of Our Lord—how to *prove*, as it were, that we have begun to appreciate it and are grateful for His suffering and death for us.

Every other matter we may like to occupy ourselves with—"political theology" and church-state relations, corruption in the hierarchy, the putative decline of culture and society, the latest twisted fads, liturgical abuses, theological controversies—these, by comparison, are distractions. We are fundamentally unjust, in Plato's terms, as we do not "mind our own work" first of all.

What I mean is this. Love is repaid by love: anyone who properly views the Passion and has a human heart will naturally be led to want to do something extravagant in response, even to give up his own life similarly. Yet *how* do we do this?

That we should—and should want to—reciprocate is echoed again and again in the saints. "O my dear Lord!" Saint Alphonsus Liguori writes, "Thou didst die in order to gain my soul; but what have I done in order to gain Thee, O infinite good?"[1] And again: "O my beloved Redeemer, Thou hast for love given Thyself wholly unto me;

[1] Alphonsus Maria de Liguori, *The Passion and the Death of Jesus Christ*, ed. Eugene Grimm (Brooklyn: Redemptorist Fathers, 1927), chap. 16, sec. 3, p. 153.

for love I give myself wholly unto Thee. Thou for my salvation hast given Thy life; I for Thy glory wish to die, when and as Thou dost please."[2] The fundamental logical inference for a Christian is this: "You died for me; I want to die for you."

Is it too much to say that if we have not in Lent and Holy Week even once felt bewildered about how we could possibly in gratitude repay, those great seasons were lost on us?

Saint Alphonsus in the same meditation tells of Blessed Henry Suso, who "one day took a knife and cut out in letters upon his breast the name of his beloved Lord. And when thus bathed in blood, he went into the church, and, prostrating himself before the crucifix, he said, 'Behold, O Lord, Thou only Love of my soul, behold my desire, I would gladly have written Thee deeper within my heart; but this I cannot do.'" Much to be preferred over tattoos and piercings.

I knew a brilliant theoretical physicist, then a graduate student at Harvard, who attempted to be as consistent in his Christianity, he thought, as in his physics. If "the Son of Man had nowhere to lay His head", neither then would he: he slept in the city park, like a homeless person, under a bench on the ground, not on it. Yes, some have also entertained theoretical physicists unawares.

I take it that many priests or religious do something like this, although not in as dramatic or outwardly romantic a fashion. They really do leave everything and offer up their own lives as an oblation. They are as good as dead from the moment they take their vows.

But what about a layperson? A layperson might look at and envy a monk. What can *he* do? He is constrained to

<hr/>

[2] Ibid., chap. 16, sec. 1, p. 150.

act like anyone else. As dramatic as the statement might be, it would hardly do for a surgeon, covered in dirt from a night on the ground in the local park, to show up for an operation with the bleeding letters of "JESUS" carved on his chest. Nor would his gesture likely be taken to be a witness to anything about God.

Yes, we will eventually die, and we can offer that up, yet what can we do *right now*? Because if we grasp our salvation in the Passion, it is with the greatest urgency that we will want to answer Christ's love with a corresponding love. It is not something we can put off.

In perplexities like this, we might simply ask God. "What would you have us do, to prove our gratitude for the Passion?" The oldest answer has been: "Repent, and be baptized" (Acts 2:38). Repent, because one can hardly be grateful for the Passion if one continues to be a cause of it, which is what any sin is. Be baptized, because such is the fundamental mode of reciprocal death that Christ asks of us, a sharing in His own death.

Baptism is "soft". It is not itself a bloody martyrdom. It includes no scourging or beatings, no hard works: "I desire mercy, and not sacrifice" (Mt 9:13). It is something material done with belief: "This is the work of God, that you believe in him whom he has sent" (Jn 6:29). We might want to carve letters in our chest—good enough— but the simple direction we get, to start, is the direction given to Namaan: simply go and wash in the water (2 Kings 5:1–19).

But now assuming we have been baptized, what next? The other answer that God Himself gives us is, "Do this in remembrance of me" (Lk 22:19). Once again, Saint Alphonsus, a priest: "O God of my soul! Since Thou didst will that the object most dear to Thy heart should die for me, I offer to Thee in my own behalf that great sacrifice of himself which this Thy Son made Thee."[3] We can "match" Christ's offering of his life exactly by offering up Christ's life reciprocally in the Mass.

For a layperson, there is indeed the patient work of turning our every good over to God, such as reckoning time and money as His, not ours. But, more fundamentally, "the faithful are destined by the baptismal character for the worship of the Christian religion.... Taking part in the Eucharistic sacrifice, which is the fount and apex of the whole Christian life, they offer the Divine Victim to God, and offer themselves along with It."[4]

I am saying that we should conceive of the Mass as our fundamental act of love. We are tempted by activism, but let's be serious—and clear that the sacraments and prayer come first.

---

[3] Ibid., chap. 15, sec. 2, p. 145.
[4] Paul VI, Dogmatic Constitution on the Church *Lumen Gentium* (November 21, 1964), no. 11.

# 8

# In the Fullness of Time

A sacrament, as we learned from our catechism, is a visible sign of grace that does what it signifies. Its efficacy is bound up with its signification. Subvert the sign, and you subvert its power (for efficacious natural signs, too, like the marital embrace).

The Passion of Our Lord is similar. The holy Doctors teach that it would have been sufficient for Jesus to have shed a single drop of blood for all of the sins of all of mankind to be forgiven—if He had so chosen. Yet, rather, He freely chose to endure His Passion. And why? Because of what was thereby expressed.

"To satisfy the divine justice," Saint Alphonsus Liguori writes, "it would be enough for him to have suffered any pain; but no, he wished to submit to the most galling insults and to the sharpest pains, in order to make us comprehend the malice of our sins, and the love with which his heart was inflamed for us."[1]

Like a sacrament, then, the Passion has an essential aspect of a sign. Our Lord freely chose that our redemption would be accomplished by this specific means, which was at the same time an expression of both the gravity of sin and the depth of God's love.

---

[1] Saint Alphonsus de Liguori, *The Passion and Death of Jesus Christ*, ed. Eugene Grimm (Brooklyn: Redemptorist Fathers, 1927), p. 414.

But to be intelligible, signs need a language and context. So here arises an interesting question: What conditions were necessary for God to have been able to fashion a sign like this? It is not so easy.

Follow me here. Suppose that God had wanted to apply a remedy for sin immediately after Adam and Eve had fallen. How could He have repaired things at the start, while expressing the correct truths?

Surely Adam and Eve needed to understand the gravity of sin. They looked upon eating the fruit as something slight, maybe even good ("to become like God"). As for God's love, they suspected, as the devil suggested, that maybe God did not have their best interests at heart. What could God have done, right then, to save them, precisely through helping them understand?

He could not have sent Jesus Christ just then. How would Jesus have come into existence? If through being born to Eve, this would have expressed, rather, the levity of sin. Suppose that Jesus was created *de novo*, a mature man, perhaps fashioned like Adam out of mud. But then why should Adam and Eve ever have believed that this third being, although like them, was God?

And how would this new being manage to die for them? If He killed himself, this would express the wrong things. But Adam and Eve did not seem particularly inclined to torture or kill anyone themselves. So, presumably, if Jesus were to die for their sins, God would have needed to create another being *de novo* (this one *not* God), somehow representing themselves, tasked with torturing and killing Him.

The material, rational creation at this point—Adam and Eve, and then another pair of rational creatures, one tasked with torturing and killing the other, the other tasked with accepting it—if it expressed anything all, would teach that torture and murder were now part of Creation and that God can be malicious.

Do you see my point? We take for granted that the Lord's Passion, as depicted by a crucifix, signifies as it does. It is only through something like a miracle, however, or many miracles, that it can do so. This marvel—that it signifies and that its signification is itself God's work—has been sensed intuitively by millions of converts, who have recognized divine power already in "Jesus Christ and Him crucified".

If what happens to Jesus is to express anything about us, He needs to be one of us: He needs to be born of a woman, and yet in such a way as to make a new start. If it is to express something about the gravity of sin, what happens to Him has to be a clear expression of our sin. But since to sin is to go astray, He needs to be tortured and put to death exactly because everything good and strong about us has gone astray—our best expression of administration (Rome), our best expression of the priesthood (Judaism), our best expression of popular acclaim (the festival crowd), our best expression of friendship (His disciples).

For it to express something about God's love, He needs to be identifiable as God. He needs to be placed in a tradition that has established incommunicable signs for God, such as a name, "I am", and incommunicable acts of God, such as forgiveness and rescue (the pascal lamb). If it is to express the ultimate form of love, it has to be a genuine giving up of His life for us. That is, he must be fully open to being put to death, while doing nothing to precipitate or recklessly cause it.

And then the whole thing needs to be presented "in the manner of a sign". Not everything is like that. If I separate my pointer and middle finger by accident, or in the dark, I cannot signify "victory" or "peace". If I do so as if inadvertently, although in plain sight, it is not yet a sign—someone needs to see that I am intending to convey something.

And just try getting executed as a madman by public authorities, and see if you succeed in "saying anything" at all. Another miracle, then: the crucifixion occurred within the short time when the great secular power of Rome and the great spiritual power that was Israel coincided in one place. And another miracle: it was for Rome to provide the final condition and seal. Jesus was not simply crucified but crucified publicly, "under Pontius Pilate". In "the fullness of time", Pilate, through his use of those three great instruments of meaning, Greek, Hebrew, and Latin, as a public act made it clear to all that this death of the King of the Jews was intended as a sign.

# 9

# Circumcision for Christians

Here is an ancient idea of Catholic spirituality, which we almost never contemplate: "In him also you were circumcised with a circumcision made without hands, by putting off the body of flesh in the circumcision of Christ", Saint Paul writes (Col 2:11). Baptism is rightly understood as a circumcision that is spiritual, not fleshly. As a result, as members of Christ's Church, we can refer to ourselves, as the Jewish people once did, by metonymy, as "The Circumcision". "We are The Circumcision!—We who worship through the Spirit of God" (Phil 3:3; AT).

Unlike the earliest Christians, few of us are converts from Judaism, so we have little reason to compare our practices with Jewish traditions.

But the main reason we do not contemplate this idea, I think, is an implicit, cultural Protestantism, which has the tendency of dissolving, and dismissing from our thought, everything mysterious.

I know because I was a Protestant once. Isn't circumcision an empty and deceptive "work of the flesh"? Surely it is "an external religious practice lacking spiritual content", as the Zondervan Bible Encyclopedia puts it: "The history of circumcision illustrated one of the basic paradoxes which plague religion. Man needs symbols as a means of expressing religious faith. Repeatedly, however, the symbols have become ends in themselves.... Periodically symbols must be renewed, or discarded."[1] In that perspective, circumcision is one among many arbitrary symbols, of utilitarian value, at best.

Such is the common opinion today, but it was not always so. I was stunned to discover a different view in Saint Thomas' commentary on the great penitential Psalm 51.

David laments there, "For behold I was conceived in iniquities; and in sins did my mother conceive me" (v. 5; DR). If proof texts were possible, this single verse would establish original sin. The prophet Samuel charged the king, "You have struck down Uriah the Hittite with the sword, and have taken his wife to be your wife" (2 Sam 12:9). Yet David's sorrow is so complete that he traces his adultery and murder back to his afflicted nature.

As Saint Thomas Aquinas explains lucidly, "Here he sets forth the root of guilt. The root of all actual guilt is original sin, which is contracted from parents tainted with that sin. This tainting was in the father of David himself, and in his mother."[2]

What comes next in the commentary seems even more interesting. Like any good interpreter, Saint Thomas poses a series of questions about the verse. *Since original sin is one thing, why does David use the plurals, "iniquities" and "sins"?* Because, Thomas says, although original sin is one in *essence*, it is multiple in *power*, since it leads to many sins.

*But had not the parents of David been cleansed from original sin through circumcision, and so David would not have been conceived in (their) original sin?* Here I was astonished to find that Saint

[1] Merrill Chapin Tenney, *The Zondervan Pictorial Encyclopedia of the Bible* (Grand Rapids: Zondervan, 1975), vol. 1, A–C, "Circumcision", p. 868.

[2] Psalm 50 (51), verse 3, ad hoc, The Aquinas Translation Project, https://hosted.desales.edu/w4/philtheo/loughlin/ATP/index.html, accessed February 4, 2025.

Thomas does not deny the underlying premise! "It must be said that baptism and circumcision do cleanse the soul of original guilt." He goes on to say, however, that each newborn child needed to be circumcised anew, just as children of baptized parents need to be baptized as well, because original sin is transmitted through the generative act.

Saint Thomas discusses circumcision at length, tellingly, in his treatise on Baptism: "All authorities are agreed in saying that original sin was remitted in circumcision." Moreover, he argues, circumcision imparted sanctifying grace sufficient for avoiding sin and made its recipient fit for eternal life in heaven.

Its main difference from Baptism, then? "Baptism operates instrumentally by the power of Christ's Passion, whereas circumcision does not; therefore Baptism imprints a character that incorporates man in Christ."[3] An interesting view: circumcision is not a mere symbol, but neither is it a sign that accomplishes what it signifies.

People say that all Catholic truth is virtually contained in any single teaching. As a thought exercise, consider some of the truths reflected in this idea that circumcision remits original sin:

1. If we affirm this full, and frankly mysterious, teaching about the ancient Jewish rite, then, to distinguish Baptism from it, we are compelled to affirm that Baptism, like other sacraments, works objectively, *ex opere operato*, "from the work as done", rather than merely on the basis of subjective belief—since circumcision did that already. That is, the import of the entire sacramental system becomes plain. Alternatively, if we want to cling to a subjective view of

---

[3] *Summa Theologica* III, art. 70.

Baptism, we must say that circumcision was merely an empty symbol.

2. We are led to affirm more strongly our continuity, as Christians, with the religion of the Israelites and, thus, our solidarity with our "elder brothers and sisters". Why? Because circumcision and sacrifices were "types" of our Baptism and the Mass—not types in the sense of similarly empty symbols, but effective "types", which conveyed God's power and grace, although in different ways.

3. The vitally important truth that original sin is not a matter of poor social influences or "structures" but is "in us" and transmitted by procreation—through the father, it has been held, not the mother—is vividly brought home by the analogy of Baptism with circumcision.

4. At the same time, the fittingness of the Virgin birth becomes apparent because it would not be fitting for the Messiah to say, with David, "Behold, I was conceived in iniquities."

5. That the sacramental remedy for this wound to our nature, and separation from God, should in some sense involve the male sex distinctively—Holy Orders now, after the Incarnation, just as the circumcision then—can no longer be attributed (as critics say) to some relatively recent European bias, but will appear to be God's decision, in His Providence, deriving from the original calling of Abraham in faith, four thousand years ago.

Viewed accurately, Baptism as "the Circumcision of Christ" seems a prime example of what Cardinal Lustiger used to call "access in Christ to all the spiritual riches of Israel".

# 10

# Happy Birthday, Immortal One!

Were we created to live forever, and can we discern that? What I mean is: Can we speak of the "intention of the Creator" in what we see? All of us die. "All men are mortal" is the famous starting point of the most ironclad syllogism. We begin to die as soon as we are born, as Saint Augustine observed. Nonetheless, do we persist in sensing that, somehow, we were "not meant to die"?

To ask these questions is the same as to ask what status death holds with us. Is death a tragedy, some kind of wreckage, "not the way things were meant to be"? Or is death simply "a natural process"? But if it is a natural process, then why does it continue to shock us?

There is a famous story about the distraught, grieving father who was consoled by the Stoic philosopher: "Did you suppose that your son was going to live forever?" Maybe he half did, even though that is not "reasonable".

We are not shocked, it is not a tragedy, when someone drops a glass and it breaks. But what is more fragile than the life of any animal?

So many things flood in when I consider these thoughts. What is it to be youthful except to embrace a hope that life has no end? Do we not see this clearly when we look, for instance, at *The Diary of Anne Frank*? We feel tremendous pain and pity, not simply that evil men were about to bring an end to her ordinary dreams: of adulthood, romance, and marriage.

Or, when I look at my children now, I do not see beings "set to die", but beings intended to live—without limit, I would say. And I would say this looking at them as living animals, not souls. It is a bit too easy—and it always was a false form of Christianity—to say that death is not problematic because we have immortal souls.

It may seem easy to be reconciled to the death of, say, an old woman, who has lived, maybe, ninety years and worked many years and raised a family. Perhaps all of her friends and even her children are already dead. Perhaps she is struggling now under many bodily infirmities and sufferings. Maybe she has even forgotten everyone around her. Should we not think of her, then, as finding peace in death—death as something "natural" after a full span of years?

I would argue that to think this is to presuppose, wrongly, as established and "intended", all of the steps of the decline. Think now of that same, wizened old woman as the youthful and beautiful girl she once was. Take her to be that lovely daughter or daughter of a friend you will see today. Or think of that lovely daughter as the wizened woman. Do you not feel now the injustice at ... the wreckage of what was meant to be? Not that it was her claim by right, but as if a birthright that should have held good was somehow lost?

But suppose that we *can* after all "see", although we find it typically much easier to deny, easier to want to deny, the "intention" in our creation that we were not meant to die. What then?

Then it seems that the fact that we exist already poses a certain choice for us between a kind of primitive faith in the Creator, call it "proto-faith", and a contrary attitude of resignation. In a world of "all men are mortal", this proto-faith will look like an irrational dream. And yet to those who nourish it, it will look like the precious truth, or the only basis for hope.

And then those who nurture this proto-faith might ask themselves: Does the Creator, too, recognize that death is a wreckage? Of course He does. Is He content to see His intention for us frustrated through sickness and death? Maybe He is not. Has He provided a remedy, then, or will He provide it, some kind of second creation or pathway to the renewal of His creation, some way in which He can "save" that which He intended in creating us?

You might have thought, when I was describing the sense we may have that "we are not meant to die", that I was appealing to some vestige of Christian culture that still survives within you and within others. Pope Benedict XVI described very well the world without Christ at the beginning of *Spe Salvi*: "No hope emerged from their contradictory myths. Notwithstanding their gods, they were 'without God' and consequently found themselves in a dark world, facing a dark future. *In nihil ab nihilo quam cito recidimus* (How quickly we fall back from nothing to nothing): so says an epitaph of that period (*Corpus Inscriptionum Latinarum* VI, no. 26003)." We may grant that such hopelessness was dominant. And yet, if it were the last and only word, then no one would have embraced Christianity.

Such is the lesson that I draw at any rate from studying the earlier Church Fathers, such as Saint Irenaeus or Saint Athanasius in his short treatise on the reasons God took on human nature, *De Incarnatione*.

Athanasius provides a good example for us. Scholars now believe he wrote this famous defense of the faith after the eruption of the Arian controversy, surely a worse "crisis in the Church" than any we face today. And yet he addresses his Jewish and Gentile readers as if the division simply did not exist.

It is the message of the Gospel that preoccupies him. The intention of the good God in creating the "race of rational creatures" would have been frustrated had He permitted us so quickly to decline into nothingness, through our sin and deliberate ignorance. Therefore, "God became man, so that man might become God", restoring the immortality that was part of the original design.

Happy birthday, then—and I mean your Baptism.

Part II

The Shock of Holiness

# "Yes" (The Holy Ulma Family)

Two thousand years ago God walked around Judea and told a parable about a despised Samaritan who assists "a man"—it could be any man—who was attacked by robbers, stripped of his clothes, and beaten nearly to death. Saint Luke, perhaps hearing the parable from Mary herself, did us the great favor of writing it down.

About eighty years ago the mother and father of a large Catholic family in a small farming village in Poland were reading that same parable. They underlined its title, "The Good Samaritan". They underlined the verses: "But a Samaritan, as he journeyed, came to where he was; and when he saw him, he had compassion, and went to him and bound up his wounds, pouring on oil and wine; then he set him on his own beast and brought him to an inn, and took care of him" (Lk 10:33–34). And then they wrote in pencil in the margin, "Yes." And this, my friends, is how Christianity works.

This mother and father were Józéf and Wiktoria Ulma. Presumably they wrote "Yes" when, in the summer of 1942, they resolved, along with their six children, that they would hide Jewish families on their farm to protect them from the Nazis.

They took in as many as their farm could accommodate: according to the Yad Vashem, the entire Szall family (father, mother, four adult sons), the two daughters of Chaim

Goldman, and the small daughter of one of these women. The Ulmas themselves lived in a small one-story house that Joséf had built. Their Jewish neighbors lived in the attic above. They undertook this risk as a family since, as they knew, if they were caught, all of them would be sent to a death camp.

For two years they succeeded. But after they were denounced (perhaps by a fellow Pole), German police descended upon the farm in the pre-dawn hours on the morning of March 24, 1944. They shot Jozéf and Wiktoria and the Jewish families immediately. After this, they conscripted witnesses from the town to see the gruesome proof of the massacre. And then they shot the Ulma children, "so that they would not be of trouble to anyone", a German police officer said after the fact.

"During the shooting, one could hear terrible cries and lamentations. The children called their parents, and they had already been killed", one witness said. A man who shot some of the children remarked, "Look how the Polish pigs that have hidden the Jews are dying."

Wiktoria was expecting and near term. She either went into labor during the executions or her body delivered the baby after death (a so-called "coffin birth"), because when her remains were exhumed, it was discovered that her child was partially born, its head and torso appearing from the birth canal. According to the postulator, Father Witold Burda, the remains were too decomposed to discover the sex of the baby.

The Ulma family was beatified on September 10, 2023, in their village of Markowa. Their feast day is Jozéf and Wiktoria's wedding anniversary, July 7.

Some observations:

- They were a large family, with seven children. Jozéf married Wiktoria in 1935, when he was thirty-five and she twenty-three. They had six children before she turned thirty. One must posit a direct connection between (a) their death to self and openness to life, shown in their generous acceptance of children, and (b) their heroic actions during the war. Stunningly, they conceived their seventh child in the darkest days of the Nazi occupation and while they were sheltering Jews at peril to themselves. That unborn baby is a great witness to their love. "The baby was trying to come into the world", Father Burda remarked.

- Their martyrdom was on the vigil of the Annunciation, as Saint Maximilian Kolbe's was on the vigil of the Assumption, a "kiss" from their Mother.

- Some want to know—is this seventh child, also Blessed, an unborn child? By this they mean, did he die while not yet born and is counted a martyr? It seems likely that this is so and that he was delivered stillborn, especially if Wiktoria was only in her seventh month, as some sources report.

- The name of this child was presumably not known even to the parents. Wiktoria was close enough to term that they would have picked out a name for a son and a name for a daughter, but in those days, they would not have known which. Indeed, now they do know. Through the couple's death, their child received a name, which they know and we do not—as if that child remains "safeguarded and sheltered" by them in their marital love.

- Wiktoria was a homemaker and Jozéf a farmer. They worked very hard on building up the "substance" of their family, saving to purchase a larger farm and improving the lands and buildings constantly. No "greed" in such industriousness! Jozéf especially was very involved in the "civil society" of his town, as a librarian, devoted photographer (then still a new

technology), and active member of the Catholic
Youth Association. Their love of Life was a love also
of being alive. As Father Burda put it: "They were
not looking for some other reality, not running away
from the world, but instead immersed in it. Through
such a way of life, they all the more discovered the
beauty and depth of their everyday life." It was because they wanted to live that they risked death. They
were not morose, escapist, or implicitly suicidal:
"They very much wanted to live," Father Burda said,
"constantly discovering the Lord God, the beauty of
everyday life, the beauty of life."

Another teaching of the Lord, then, to which they said
"Yes": "He who loses his life for my sake will find it" (Mt
10:39).

Heroes who have received the Congressional Medal of
Honor (not posthumously) will typically say "I did only
what anyone else would do" and "Many others did the
same who will never be known." Canonized saints and
the blessed are just like this.

Let us, like the Ulmas, in the presence of "the Father
who sees in secret", find a verse in the Gospel to live by
and structure our lives around a similar "yes".

12

# Consider Saint John Vianney

In the summer of 1859, the Pike's Peak Gold Rush began. Amherst and Williams played the very first intercollegiate baseball game. In October, John Brown raided Harper's Ferry. Troops commanded by Robert E. Lee captured him. He would be hanged on December 2. And, on August 4 of that same year, the Curé of Ars, Jean Baptiste Vianney, died in his village in France, age seventy-three.

Vianney's beatification and canonization were among the most rapid in modern times, before the reforms in these processes by Pope John Paul II. Pope Pius X beatified him in 1905, and on May 31, 1925, he was canonized a saint by Pius XI.

Saint Josemaria Escrivá famously remarked that "these world crises are crises of saints."[1] We may heartily agree with the statement and yet not quite understand precisely what it means. What it means seems to vary as much with the individual, and the crisis, as does sanctity itself. Consider as pertinent examples: Saints Juan Diego, Thomas More, John Henry Newman, Mother Teresa, and John Paul II. But for us, now, let's consider Vianney.

In retrospect, Vianney looks to be one of several great priests and religious raised up in the wake of the French

[1] Josemaria Escriva, *The Way: The Essential Classic of Opus Dei's Founder* (New York: Penguin Random House, 2006), p. 51.

Revolution to help bring France back to the faith. He was a boy during the French Revolution and Reign of Terror. He saw priests executed and the churches closed under order of civil authorities. Yet for him, the need for priests became, therefore, more palpable, not less so. And he was not alone: among those ordained deacons with him in Lyons were Marcellin Champagnat (canonized a saint by John Paul II in 1999) and Jean-Claude Colin, founder of the Marist Fathers.

Yet although saints are the answer to crises, they do not aspire to be "answers to crises"—nor arguably could they become saints if they did so. They aspire to love God passionately, regardless of crises. Vianney's biographer, Joseph Vianney, interprets Vianney's well-known struggles with Latin and philosophy in this light.

By human lights, Joseph writes, one might have thought that the crisis in France would best be answered by brilliant apologetics in the Sorbonne or attractive oratory in the cathedral of Notre Dame. But the Church had still greater need of country pastors, "to demonstrate, by the sanctity of their lives, the truth of the Gospel, in which the people had ceased to believe. The child from Dardilly had been chosen, from among all others, to be the model of those holy priests who are indispensable to the execution of the divine plan."[2]

Late in life a churchman brought a complex case of conscience to the confessional in Ars for the Curé's counsel and found that a problem that had perplexed the greatest moral theologians was resolved immediately, elegantly, and convincingly by the simple pastor. He asked where Vianney had acquired such astute theological knowledge. The saint responded by pointing to his prie-dieu.

---

[2] Joseph Vianney, *The Blessed John Vianney: Curé d'Ars, Patron of Parish Priests*, trans. C.W.W. (London: Duckworth, 1906), p. 15.

The Curé was deeply convinced of his own unworthiness, received no consolations from his own virtue, and prayed fervently that no attention would ever be drawn to him. For instance, through his prayers, thousands of pilgrims to Ars were cured of bodily ailments. But apparently, in answer to his prayers, they were almost never cured on the spot. Rather, he would tell them to go back home and make a novena to Saint Philomena—and on the ninth day they would be cured, without attention, and far from Ars.

It is well known that he would spend sixteen or seventeen hours in the confessional each day. That figure itself seems sufficiently impressive. But then consider that his church was not heated. He would quip humorously that, at the end of the day in the winter, he would see his feet first, before he could feel them. He would touch them, he said, to reassure himself they were still there.

In the high heat of summer, yes, the pilgrims waiting in line could step outside for a moment and get fresh air to avoid fainting. But he spent the whole time behind a curtain in a box fed by the breath of the penitents, and often, as they were mainly poor, by their odor, too. And then he listened to sins during those sixteen or seventeen hours. This was his greatest cause of suffering. "I pine away with melancholy on this wretched earth", he once told a fellow priest, "my soul is sad even unto death. My ears hear nothing but painful things that break my heart with grief." His biographer writes that this was as if Saint Peter had been compelled to witness the Passion for seventeen hours each day, day after day.[3]

He slept on boards for just a few hours nightly, enduring chronic pain. Only grace and love can explain his energy during the day. He consumed too little food for anyone to live on by natural means. Late in life, under obedience, he would take a little bread and milk after Mass. His biographer gives this telling incident: "Brother Jerome, who was often present at this light repast, soon noticed that he always ate the bread first, and drank the milk afterward. 'But, Monsieur le Curé,' he observed one day when he saw with what difficulty the bread was swallowed, 'if you were to put your bread in the milk it would be much better.' 'Yes, I know' was his gentle answer."[4]

And, as he himself would say, things were much more difficult for a parish priest than a religious: "It is thought, prayer, intimate union with God that a priest needs. The curé, however, lives in the world; he converses, mixes in politics, reads the newspapers, has his head full of them; then he goes to read his breviary, and say his Mass; and so, alas! he does it as if it were an ordinary thing!"[5]

Alas indeed! His words apply to laypersons as well as secular priests. *And these world crises are crises of saints.* And you, and your life?

[4] Ibid., p. 177.
[5] Ibid., pp. 181–82.

# 13

# Saint Thomas More's Epitaph

I want to consider with you the epitaph that Saint Thomas More wrote for his own tomb (in Chelsea) in the summer of 1532, three years before his death—which is to say, before his imprisonment but just after he resigned as lord chancellor. He wrote it in Latin prose, but it concludes with ten lines in verse. It is a minor masterpiece, about seven hundred words in translation.

An epitaph (literally "placed on a tomb") written for oneself is a strange genre. It seems to offer an assessment of your life as if from God's point of view. Thus, any vanity or posturing will be immediately clear to others, although the author may be blind to it. Moreover, to be genuine, it must be the fruit of interiority, of self-examination in the presence of God. Yet it is difficult for something so intimate to be publicly shared.

More avoids any such posturing and falseness by framing his life as if from both sides, youth and old age, from the point of view of two fathers. After an opening paragraph, where he recounts matter-of-factly his accomplishments and office, he memorializes his father. Thus, he makes it clear that, from his youth, he had lived his life to please the good intentions of his earthly father:

When he had thus gone through this course of offices or honours, that neither that gracious prince could disallow

67

his doings, nor he was odious to the nobility nor unpleasant to the people, but yet to thieves, murderers and heretics grievous, at last John More, his father, knight, and chosen of the prince to be one of the justices of the King's Bench, a civil man, pleasant, harmless, gentle, pitiful, just and un-corrupted, in years old, but in body more than for his years lusty, after that he perceived his life so long lengthened, that he saw his son lord chancellor of England, thinking himself now to have lived long enough, gladly departed to God.[1]

Yes, we need to read this paragraph understanding that we are not to be scandalized that he thought it right to censure heretics. We need, too, to be familiar with older English us-ages: "disallow" here means "fail to accept with pleasure"; and "lusty" means "vigorous, strong". And then we cannot fail to notice More's characteristic good humor, such as saying that he was odious to the right sorts of persons, or, as we would say, "You need to have the right enemies."

But besides being a gracious way of thanking and hon-oring his father, this passage is used by More to personalize his career, as if to say, *if in another life his father had been glad that he himself had been a simple tradesman, More would have been content in that as well*—just as wise persons today give the advice, to those facing a career choice, "What would make your parents happy?"

Next in the epitaph comes what I regard as its most as-tonishing detail, a confession of how More viewed his own life, which testifies that he is writing out of intimate self-knowledge. When his father died, he changed from viewing himself as a young man to viewing himself as an old man:

[1] T.E. Bridgett, *Life and Writings of Sir Thomas More* (London: Burns & Oates, 1892), pp. 250–52.

His son then, his father being dead, to whom as long as he lived being compared was wont both to be called young and himself so thought too, missing now his father departed, and seeing four children of his own, and of their offspring eleven, began in his own conceit to wax old; and this affection of his was increased by a certain sickly disposition of his breast, even by and by following, as a sign or token of age creeping upon him. He, therefore, irked and weary of worldly business, giving up his promotions, obtained at last by the incomparable benefit of his most gentle prince, if it please God to favour his enterprise, the thing which from a child in a manner always he wished and desired: that he might have some years of his life free, in which he little and little withdrawing himself from the business of this life, might continually remember the immortality of the life to come.[2]

He missed his father, lost his youth, and began to notice something within him, calling him out of this life as well. And yet this new stage, too, was continuous, as it was "the thing which from a child in a manner always he wished and desired". This was More the young child living without care in the sight of his Father, God.

In the closing paragraph, he tells the meaning of his tomb: that it "every day put him in memory of death that never ceases to creep on him". He then asks anyone who reads the inscription to pray for him "that this tomb made for him in his lifetime be not in vain, nor that he fear death coming upon him, but that he may willingly, for the desire of Christ, die and find death not utterly death to him, but the gate of a wealthier life."[3]

[2] Ibid., p. 251.
[3] Ibid.

In these lines, was More anticipating the prayers of those who might see the epitaph while More was still alive? Or did More believe that later generations passing by and reading it might efficaciously pray for him in the past, that he give good witness in the martyrdom that he expected was soon to come to him? Because of this epitaph itself, did later generations of Catholics actually assist this great saint in his last hours? We do not know.

The final lines, in touching Latin verse, are for his two wives, Jane (died early) and Alice:

> Which most my love, I know not—first or last.
> Oh! had religion destiny allowed,
> How smoothly mixed had our three fortunes flowed!
> But, be we in the tomb, in heaven allied,
> So kinder death shall grant what life denied.[4]

Had religion allowed destiny, too, that we and More had lived in the same age! But let us pray that kinder death shall grant what life denied, and that, as the saint liked to say about heaven, we shall "make merry together" with him throughout eternity.

[4] Ibid., p. 252.

# 14

# Saint Jean's Two Martyrdoms
## (Saint Jean de Brébeuf)

When an exact replica of the Shroud of Turin was put on display at the Catholic Information Center (CIC) in Washington, D.C., courtesy of the Museum of the Bible, Father Charles Trullols of the CIC commented: "The Shroud reminds us that we need to keep the message of Ash Wednesday imprinted on our souls, as we contemplate the imprint of the suffering of Our Lord on the Shroud. We also need to help Jesus with His Cross, with his sufferings."[1]

It was Lent, and, while contemplating those words, I do not know why, but I was drawn to thinking about the martyrdom of Saint Jean de Brébeuf. I looked up the original report in the Jesuit *Relations*, based on the testimony of two Huron Indians the day after, who had witnessed it and escaped.

They tore out his nails to start. Then they beat him fiercely with cudgels, about two hundred blows, over his loins, belly, legs, and face: "Although Father de Brébeuf was overwhelmed under the weight of these blows, he did

---

[1] Father Charles Trullols, "Ash Wednesday 2023 Reflections", March 12, 2023, YouTube, https://youtu.be/zINTHhQei2w?si=gWaiKWaX2-HOLF0T (site no longer active).

not cease continually to speak of God, and to encourage all the new Christians who were captives like himself to suffer well, that they might die well, in order to go in company with him to Paradise."[2]

Next, an Iroquois responded with a mock baptism, pouring boiling water over him three times: "'Echon', that is Father de Brébeuf's name in Huron, 'thou sayest that Baptism and the sufferings of this life lead straight to Paradise; thou wilt go soon, for I am going to baptize thee, and to make thee suffer well, in order to go the sooner to thy Paradise.'"[3]

Then, they placed upon him a collar of six red hot hatchets.

> I have seen no torment which more moved me to compassion than that. For you see a man, bound naked to a post, who, having this collar on his neck, cannot tell what posture to take. For, if he lean forward, those above his shoulders weigh the more on him; if he lean back, those on his stomach make him suffer the same torment; if he keep erect, without leaning to one side or other, the burning hatchets, applied equally on both sides, give him a double torture.

After that, they wrapped around his waist a belt stuffed with highly flammable pitch and resin and lit it on fire, "which roasted his whole body". Throughout, "Father de Brébeuf endured like a rock, insensible to fire and flames, which astonished all the bloodthirsty wretches who tormented him. His zeal was so great that he preached continually to these infidels, to try to convert them."[4]

---

[2] *Jesuit Relations and Allied Documents*, vol. 34, ed. Reuben Gold Thwaites (Cleveland: Burrows Brothers Co., 1898), p. 28.

[3] Ibid.

[4] Ibid., p. 29.

Then, to keep him from speaking, they cut off his upper and lower lips. Then they flayed his legs, down to the bone, and roasted the flesh before his eyes. The mocking continued: "Thou seest plainly that we treat thee as a friend, since we shall be the cause of thy Eternal happiness; thank us, then, for these good offices which we render thee—for, the more thou shalt suffer, the more will thy God reward thee."[5]

While he was still alive but on the point of death, they carved out his heart and ate it, taking up his still warm blood to drink. They were so impressed by his courage that they wanted to become like him, through consuming him.

The Feast of the North American Martyrs, I have long known, is October 19. But on what day did Jean de Brébeuf die? I looked it up. It was March 16, 1649, during Lent. (Easter Sunday was April 4 that year.) He was captured early in the morning and died at 4 P.M., after sixteen hours of what a secular website of Canadian history calls "one of the most atrocious martyrdoms in the annals of Christianity".[6]

Such extraordinary witness does not come from nowhere. Father de Brébeuf had arrived in "New France" twenty-four years earlier. He studied with great attention first the Algonquins, then the Hurons. He was the first European to master Wendat, the Huron language, composing a dictionary, a grammar, and catechisms for the language.

He wrote the famous "Huron Carol" in Wendat, although his actual words were different from versions popular today. It began not with the nostalgic "'Twas in the

[5] Ibid.

[6] "Brébeuf, Jean de", *The Dictionary of Canadian Biography*, https://www.biographi.ca/en/bio/brebeuf_jean_de_1E.html.

moon of wintertime", but rather with a stern warning not
to heed the devil:

> Have courage, you who are humans. Jesus, He is born.
> Behold, it has fled, the spirit who had us as prisoner.
> Do not listen to it, as it corrupts our minds, the spirit of
>    our thoughts.[7]

The tune that the saint used was different, too: "Une Jeune
Pucelle", which was a French folk song dating from 1557.

Jean de Brébeuf's *Spiritual Journal* reveals a man deeply
dedicated to contemplative prayer and strict in keeping
his rule, who was granted many mystical visions, some of
them accompanied by temptations from the devil. In 1631,
he made a "Vow of Service", which contains these words:
"I make a vow to you never to fail, on my side, in the
grace of martyrdom, if by your infinite mercy you offer it
to me some day, to me, your unworthy servant."[8]

But perhaps equally impressive was his bloodless martyrdom, of returning to the apostolate again and again,
over three decades, despite repeated rejections, persecu-
tions, and only a handful of conversions to show for it. Just
before his death, he wrote:

> O my God, why are you not known? Why is this bar-
> barous country not all converted to you? Why is not sin
> abolished from it? Why are you not loved? Yes, my God,
> if all the torments which the captives can endure in these

---

[7] "Huron Carol Translation with Pronunciation Guide", The Huron
Carol, last visited September 27, 2006, archived at https://web.archive.org
/web/20060927091554/http://www.rockies.net/~spirit/charlene/huroncarol1
.html.

[8] Kathleen O'Donnell, "Brébeuf's Spiritual Journal", *Canadian Literature*,
no. 53 (1972): 43.

countries in the cruelty of the tortures, were to fall on me, I offer myself thereto with all my heart, and I alone will suffer them.[9]

Why are You not loved still?—Is any other prayer, "with all my heart", more appropriate for me?

Saint Jean de Brébeuf, pray for us.

[9] Ibid., p. 44.

# 15

# Who Is Like God?
## (Saint Michael the Archangel)

*Question*: What holy place far from Rome was visited on pilgrimage by Saints Thomas Aquinas, Catherine of Siena, Bernard of Clairvaux, Francis of Assisi, and many popes, including Saint John Paul II? Perhaps you would be keen to join this illustrious company.

*Answer*: The shrine of Saint Michael in Monte Sant'Angelo, on the slopes of Mount Gargano overlooking the Adriatic, located on the "spur" of the boot which is Italy.

The shrine itself is located in a cave, an ancient site of pagan worship, where according to hagiographical tradition the archangel Michael appeared in 490. He instructed that a shrine be built to his honor and that those who invoked him would be defended in battle against pagan military incursions. Pope Gelasius I approved the shrine in 493.

I said that Saint Francis of Assisi had visited the shrine, and yet only in a manner of speaking. This great saint made the journey to Monte Sant'Angelo but considered himself too unworthy actually to enter the cave once there. It was enough for him to make the sign of a cross with his finger on a stone outside.

You may say: *I have never heard of this great place of pilgrimage*. Neither had I, until recently. But perhaps like me, from now on, you will pray for the means and opportunity to go there?

Monte Sant'Angelo is not unlike Mont-Saint-Michel on the other side of Europe, founded in the early 800s after Saint Michael appeared there, too, and instructed the bishop to build him a shrine. These shrines together illustrate four important marks about devotion to Saint Michael: *antiquity*, *exogeneity*, *catholicity*, and *urgency*.

First, *antiquity*. Devotion to Saint Michael is something I would have once scratched my head over, when I first converted and was an "Evangelical Protestant". After all, it is not something that, on Protestant principles, *ought* to exist, in its picture of "early Christianity". And yet there it is, from the beginning. At least it is manifested as soon as Christianity is manifested publicly. Around 324, the Emperor Constantine built the "Michaelion", a church in honor of the angel, after Saint Michael appeared to him and helped him win a battle. The iconography of Saint Michael as a soldier slaying the serpent Satan dates from this time. But historians believe that Constantine was simply affirming publicly a tradition of devotion that was already centuries old.

Second, *exogeneity*. That is a fancy word that economists use for causes that come "from outside" a system. It is a fact that devotion to Saint Michael from the beginning has been construed within pious tradition, not as a construct or invention of human piety, but as a response to particular interventions of the angel from without. The angel is sensed as a supernatural person who manifests himself, without warning, and who gives definite instructions to Christians to honor him in certain places. The famous Saint Michael prayer of Pope Leo XIII, somewhat similarly, was composed by that great pontiff after he fainted from an oppressive vision of besetting demons.[1]

Third, *catholicity*. By this I mean in part that devotion to Saint Michael has erupted throughout Christendom. But also that, by God's design, apparently, this devotion has been wont to "take over" pagan devotion. The cave of Monte Sant'Angelo was a place of pagan worship. In Germany, shrines to Saint Michael supplanted places that had previously been devoted to the Norse God, Odin ("Wotan"). It is as if people sensed that what was found alluring in the false god was found, truly, in the goodness of that mighty angel.

Saint Michael has a particular appeal to the human imagination generally. I have noticed this directly in my own life. Once a sculptor friend, not a Catholic or even a Christian, but inspired by the example of a young Catholic family in what can often seem a hostile world, made a statue for me to honor my namesake. He crafted it so that, looked at one way, it was a mighty angel with a sword, and, looked at another way, it appeared as a child shielded by the presence of his parents.

My friend had thus, unbeknownst to himself, captured in a single work the two offices traditionally ascribed to Saint Michael: the first, better-known office is that he fights spiritual battles; the second, hardly known at all, is that he has been regarded from the earliest centuries of the Church as a great healer and salve.

The fourth mark is, finally, *urgency*. "It is true that 'the powers of death shall not prevail,' as the Lord has assured (Mt 16:18), but this does not mean that we are exempt from trials and battles against the snares of the evil one", as

---

[1] See the excellent book by Kevin Symonds, *Pope Leo XIII and the Prayer to St. Michael* (Boonville, N.Y.: Preserving Christian Publications, 2018).

Saint John Paul II said, when he visited Monte Sant'Angelo, explaining how prayers to Saint Michael have a certain urgency in every age.

Note that the prayer of exorcism, which Leo XIII composed as a companion to the Saint Michael prayer and which he himself recited many times each day, refers to devils that have *already* besieged the holiest places—during a pontificate some look back upon now with nostalgia:

> This battle against the devil which characterizes the Archangel Michael remains relevant today, because the devil is still alive and at work in the world. In fact, the evil that is in it, the disorder we see in society, the incoherence of man, the interior fragmentation of which he is a victim, are not merely the consequences of original sin, but also the effect of the dark and infesting activity of Satan, of this saboteur of man's moral equilibrium. St Paul does not hesitate to call him "the god of this world" (2 Cor 4:4), inasmuch as he shows himself to be a cunning enchanter, who knows how to insinuate himself into our actions so as to introduce deviations which are as destructive as they are apparently conformed to our instinctive aspirations.[2]

Thus, again, words of Saint John Paul II. I know no better description of the urgency of spiritual combat today, for which Saint Michael is the catholic remedy.

> *V. Behold the Cross of the Lord, flee bands of enemies.*
> *R. The Lion of the tribe of Juda, the offspring of David,*
> *hath conquered.*[3]

---

[2] Pope St. John Paul II, Address to the Citizens of Monte Sant'Angelo (May 24, 1987), https://www.vatican.va/content/john-paul-ii/it/speeches/1987/may/documents/hf_jp-ii_spe_19870524_monte-sant-angelo.html.

[3] From Pope Leo XIII's prayer of exorcism. Quoted in Symonds, *Pope Leo XIII and the Prayer to St. Michael.*

# 16

# What Saint Thomas Aquinas
# Did Not Say

It was most likely on December 6, 1273, one might sur-
mise from the best accounts, that a brother in the Order
of Preachers (the Dominicans) named Dominic of Caserta,
who was serving as sacristan at the priory at Naples, sneaked
into the chapel of Saint Nicholas to see if *he* was there once
more—that is to say, Thomas Aquinas, who, as this brother
had many times observed before, liked to leave his room
secretly before Matins and quietly descend the stairs to the
church, in order to pray before the others arrived.

Matins for the early Dominicans was at 3:00 A.M., so we
are talking about perhaps two in the morning. It would
have been very dark and cold.

On this occasion, however, Nicholas did not simply
glance in the chapel to confirm the saint's presence, as he
would usually do, but, for some reason or other, he decided to peer in and look with greater care. What he saw
astounded him: Thomas, turned toward a crucifix in an
attitude of prayer, was suspended in the air about three feet
above the ground, apparently oblivious to the fact that he
was levitating.

He was aware that others in the order had spoken of
the phenomenon already. In particular, a *socius* of Thomas,

Reginald, and a certain brother James had witnessed the saint become lifted about five feet off the ground at the high altar once after Matins. But Dominic was so amazed that he kept looking on in wonderment and awe—for how long he did not quite know.

Then, suddenly, he heard a voice, very clear and articulate, coming from the crucifix and speaking to the saint: "You have written well of me, Thomas. What compensation, therefore, would you like to receive for this your work?"

He then heard the saint say in reply . . .

Well, what *did* Saint Thomas say? It is a popular story, repeated thousands of times. You probably have heard it. The background for the story, given above, I have taken directly from one of the earliest lives of Saint Thomas, composed by Bernard of Gui in 1318 for the canonization proceedings, about forty-five years after the saint's passing. I am guessing you did not know that his biographer included the story as much for its witness to the saint's levitation as for the famous colloquy with Our Lord in the crucifix.

I am also guessing you do not know the saint's words. In those popular accounts, we are told that Saint Thomas said, *Domine, non nisi te.* Also, we are told that these words mean, "Lord, nothing except you." But Bernard of Gui gives different words. He reports Saint Thomas as saying, "Lord, I would not accept another compensation, without you yourself." (In Latin: *Domine, non aliam mercedem recipiam, nisi teipsum.*)[1]

The difference is significant. In the popular accounts, Saint Thomas is saying that he wants and expects no

---

[1] Bernard Gui, *Vita Sancti Thomae Aquinatis, in Fontes vitae S. Thomae Aquinatis: Notis historicis et criticis illustrati*, ed. D. Prümmer (Toulouse: [n.p.], 1912), 189.

compensation, that the possession of Our Lord is enough—call it "Saint Thomas the Personalist", or maybe even "Saint Thomas the Kantian". In Gui's telling, by contrast, Saint Thomas is saying that he would be pleased with compensation. It even seems to imply that he was hoping for it. But he says that he would not be satisfied with any compensation that did not include the possession of the Lord himself. In brief, it is a difference in whether the concept of merit, and of heavenly reward along the lines of wages earned, enters into Saint Thomas' thought or not.

It is something like the difference between: Your wife asks what cake you would like for your birthday, and you say either (1) I do not want a cake; all I want is you; or (2) I do not want a cake except one that you are baking for me and serving to me.

Gui goes on to explain the colloquy in a way that definitely supports the second mode of interpretation:

> Thomas had been writing at the time the third and last part of the *Summa theologiae*, where he had been dealing with the Incarnation, birth, Passion, and resurrection of Christ.... Since the Lord had posed this question about compensation, he was given to understand that his recent labor would mark the end of his work. And indeed he wrote little after this. Accordingly, he asked to have, as an appropriate compensation, that when he reached his homeland, he should be refreshed with the fullest savor of the One by whom, on this way of pilgrimage, his life had been sweetened with such sweetness.[2]

Gui's explanation uses language apparently drawn from Saint Thomas' Eucharistic hymns, especially *Adoro Te Devote*.

And none of this is surprising if one looks at Saint Thomas' own discussion of merit in the *Summa* (I-II, q. 114).

---

[2] Ibid.

But we can be absolutely certain that if Thomas' words were indeed *Domini, non nisi te* (as William of Tocco, another earlier biographer, has it), these words do *not* mean "Lord, nothing except you." *Non* is a negative; it requires a verb to negate. *Non* is not a substantive, *nihil*, "nothing". In the over eighty occurrences of *non nisi* in the *Summa*, it always means "not without", and "not" picks up a verb.

Without doubt, then, Gui states the meaning correctly. The versions are disparate only because Tocco wrote with compression, relying on the context to fill out the meaning, or Gui expanded Saint Thomas' terse reply, correctly explaining its meaning, given the question. Those hundreds of versions on the internet posted by bishops, Dominicans, and even classical academies, explaining "*non nisi te*" as "nothing except you", are all wrong.

Some lessons to draw from all this? Learn Latin, to consult primary sources yourself. Do not put too much stock on stories repeated on the internet, and taken from there to embellish sermons and dinner speeches. The true story with its craggy details will always be more interesting.

But, above all, imitate Saint Thomas as best we can in prayer, Eucharistic devotion, and hope of heavenly reward.

*Iesu, quem velatum nunc aspicio, oro fiat illud quod tam sitio; ut te revelata cernens facie, visu sim beatus tuae gloriae. Amen.*

Contemplating, Lord, Thy hidden presence, grant me what I thirst for and implore, in the revelation of Thy essence to behold Thy glory evermore. Amen.[3]

[3] Taken from the translation of the "Adoro te Devote" first published in *The Irish Monthly*, vol. 5, p. 295, attributed there to "J.O'H", who has since been identified as Judge John O'Hagan.

# 17

# Witnesses to a Proper Fear
## (The Martyrs of Compiègne)

There are important respects in which any martyr is important for our time. But are there some more relevant than others? If so, which are most relevant—and why?

You may be familiar with the fascinating passages in *Veritatis Splendor* where Saint Pope John Paul II teaches that false views of ethics are refuted by the witness of any martyr:

> The unacceptability of "teleological", "consequentialist" and "proportionalist" ethical theories, which deny the existence of negative moral norms regarding specific kinds of behaviour, norms which are valid without exception, is confirmed in a particularly eloquent way by Christian martyrdom, which has always accompanied and continues to accompany the life of the Church even today (no. 90).

This great pope, who had seen many martyrs to Communism and Nazism, taught the essential connection between life in Christ and martyrdom—and warned the Church to be prepared (in the right way) to give witness to the faith in death.

And yet it seems that some martyrs are more relevant than others. The North American martyrs are more relevant to us because they are close to us: their Our Lady of Martyrs

84

Shrine is a stop on the New York State Thruway. Lawyers and politicians rightly find Saint Thomas More highly relevant. Saint Maria Goretti and the early Roman virgin-martyrs will seem relevant whenever a Christian must accept sacrifices rather than go along with an eroticized culture. But these are examples of martyrs for special places, circumstances, and occupations. What is the standard, common, and perduring situation of a Christian today? Considered historically, surely, it is being embedded within modern, secular societies, that is to say, "liberal regimes". For someone so situated, arguably the most important martyrs for us are the sixteen Carmelite sisters from Compiègne, executed by guillotine in 1794 in the Place de la Nation in Paris, during the Reign of Terror of the French Revolution.

At least, so it has been argued by Christians of the highest religious and artistic sensibility. I mean Gertrud von Le Fort, in her novella, *Song at the Scaffold*. And Georges Bernanos, who wrote a play based on the novella, titled *Dialogues des Carmélites*. And Francis Poulenc, whose 1956 opera of the same title is based on a libretto by Bernanos.

Almost every account of martyrdom is graced by details that are deeply moving if they come to light. In the case of "the Martyrs of Compiègne", the prioress stood at the base of the scaffold, holding a small statue of Madonna and Child, which each sister kissed, before the exchange: "Permission to die, Mother?"—"Go, my daughter!"

One elderly nun, Sister Charlotte, unable to walk without a cane, was thrown roughly from the cart by a guard: she lay face down, it seemed dead, but then stirred and, getting up, gave thanks that she was still alive, able to die as a martyr with her sisters.

The nun who went first, one of the youngest, Sister Constance, as she approached the guillotine broke out into song with the *Salve Regina* from Compline. The other sisters joined in, as if in choir. Next the *Te Deum* and *Laudate Dominum*, with the sound trailing off as the sisters fell, one by one. The mob gathered there, usually shouting obscenities and curses, this time was completely silent.

More than a year earlier, in September 1792, the sisters at the initiative of the prioress had made an act of consecration of martyrdom, "so that peace may be restored to the Church and the state".[1] The fact that, only ten days after their execution, the Reign of Terror came to an abrupt and unexpected end was taken even then as a sign that their wish had been generously granted by God.

But as I said, these details, astonishing as they are, do not set apart this martyrdom as being especially relevant for us, because all martyrdoms are like this. Rather, one needs to view this martyrdom interiorly and spiritually, not neglecting its political context.

And this is the great service that von le Fort, Bernanos, and Poulenc provide us, in their exploration of how entire societies may be manipulated by fear, and of what is required for acting with dignity in the midst of widespread fear. Is fear something we should show contempt for or embrace? Are there different kinds of fear, such that one kind, which is good, helps drive out others, which are bad?

Von le Fort wrote in 1931, when the clouds of Nazi totalitarianism were beginning to gather; Bernanos and Poulenc, in the ruins of World War II and its camps. They agreed in finding the witness of the nuns prophetic—warning that the ideals of liberty, equality, and fraternity, if accompanied by irreverence and hatred of religion, can easily be transmogrified into their opposites.

[1] "Blessed: The True Story of the Carmelite Martyrs of Compiègne", by De Grand Matin Productions, YouTube, April 2, 2025, https://www.youtube.com/watch?v=nDKBFFA-2XM.

To explore fear, von le Fort placed at the center of her novel a fictional sister dominated by fear, Sister Blanche, whom she contrasts with a courageous sister, Marie of the Incarnation, who acts with heroism, sometimes almost recklessly it seems, in contempt of fear. Von le Fort clearly believes that the way for a Christian in a "post-Christian society" is to be united with Christ in the precise fear He showed in the garden.

"My friend, fear is a great emotion", a character says in her novel, looking back at the Terror. But then she adds, strikingly, "Not one of us was sufficiently afraid! Society should be afraid. A State should know fear. Governments should tremble. To tremble is to be strong. These things I am writing of have taken place and may reoccur at any moment!"[2]

What Von le Fort feared—she, almost alone among Germans—did indeed reoccur. It recurred from a lack of the requisite fear. Have we learned her lesson? Do we even look to where we might learn it?

Martyrs of the Compiègne, teach us a holy fear, and pray for us!

---

[2] Gertrude von le Fort, *The Song at the Scaffold* (San Francisco: Ignatius Press, 2011), p. 79.

# 18

# Dies Natalis
# (Saint Stephen and Saint Fulgentius)

Today, the day after Christmas,[1] the Church celebrates the feast of Saint Stephen, the "Protomartyr", meaning both someone first in time and one who serves as an example to us all.

One might wonder, why? We are in the "Octave of Christmas", after all. What does Stephen's martyrdom have to do with the birth of Christ?

The Office of Readings for the day contains a sermon by the sixth-century bishop Saint Fulgentius, which explains why. Fulgentius is one of those little-known saints whom one is simply astonished to learn about. (But all the saints are like that.) Can such a man have lived?

He was taught Greek first, before Latin, so that he would be able to pronounce it flawlessly. As a boy, he committed the entire *Iliad* and *Odyssey* to memory. He turned to monastic life after encountering Saint Augustine's commentary on Psalm 36. He spent his adult life looking (always prudently) for a stricter and more austere rule of life, while suffering persecution and exile by Arians.

He was so revered for learning and holiness that once when he showed up at a monastery, the abbot resigned and said Fulgentius deserved to be abbot instead. Or when

---

[1] Published on *The Catholic Thing*, December 26, 2018.

contrary winds once kept his boat in harbor as he was being sent to exile, thousands learned about it and gathered to hear him preach and receive Communion from him.

The great Fulgentius' sermon on Saint Stephen begins, "Yesterday we celebrated the birth in time of our eternal King. Today we celebrate the triumphant suffering of his soldier", which is interesting—not least as showing that the two feasts were juxtaposed as early as the sixth century.[2]

Fulgentius draws three connections between two feasts. The first is the connection between birth and death. For a Christian, death is birth unto eternal life, as reflected in the very phrase *Dies natalis*, "birthday", to mark the date of passing of one of the faithful.

We want to imitate Christ. As Nicodemus pointed out, we cannot crawl back into the womb to be born again, imitating Him on Christmas. But we can imitate Him in dying. "Yesterday", the saint continues, "our King, clothed in his robe of flesh, left his place in the virgin's womb and graciously visited the world. Today his soldier leaves the tabernacle of his body and goes triumphantly to heaven."[3]

So, Christian, the day after Christmas, reflect on your death, and ask for the grace to die in the same joy that you share on Christmas morning, in imitation of the infant Christ.

The second connection he draws, already evident in the two quotations, is between Christ, born King, and Stephen, His soldier. This is highly interesting. We speak of the "Kingdom of God", in which God reigns as King.

But "King" is a correlative term. How do we refer to those "under" the King? Are they "citizens" in this Kingdom

---

[2] *The Liturgy of the Hours*, vol. 1 (New York: Catholic Book Publishing Co., 1975), p. 1256.
[3] Ibid.

or its "servants"? Fulgentius thinks of them as soldiers, presumably on the grounds that the subjects of a Kingdom
asked to show the most loyalty, to the point of giving up
their lives, are precisely its soldiers.

The Good News of the arrival of the Kingdom of God
is therefore also the news that we have been enlisted as
soldiers. Fulgentius' own life showed a real grasp of the
demands of spiritual combat. He rightly holds up martyrdom as the fullest and clearest expression of a Christian's
loyalty to his King.

It is said that the frankincense brought by the Wise Men
prefigures the Lord's Passion and death, but by the same
token it prefigures the martyrdom—"red", "white", or
unnoticed—to which we are called.

However, in his sermon, Fulgentius devotes most of his
attention to a third connection: of charity. The charity that
brought the Lord to earth is the same charity that brought
Stephen to heaven:

> He brought his soldiers a great gift that not only enriched
> them but also made them unconquerable in battle, for it
> was the gift of love, which was to bring men to share in
> his divinity. He gave of his bounty, yet without any loss
> to himself. In a marvelous way he changed into wealth the
> poverty of his faithful followers while remaining in full
> possession of his own inexhaustible riches. And so the love
> that brought Christ from heaven to earth raised Stephen
> from earth to heaven.[4]

This thought provides an intriguing interpretation of gift-
giving at Christmas. It is not to "celebrate" the day, or even
to give gifts to others, in order to give them to the infant
Christ. Instead, the explosion of gifts on Christmas Day

[4] Ibid.

stands as effect to cause. We are meant to see divine love in the effects—while at the same time, through gift-giving, we are meant to lead one another heavenward.

Stephen's martyrdom did this in an exemplary way. Love is a unitive force, strikingly, between him and Saul: "Love was Stephen's weapon by which he gained every battle, and so won the crown signified by his name" [*stephanos* = "crown" in Greek].

> His love of God kept him from yielding to the ferocious mob; his love for his neighbor made him pray for those who were stoning him.... Strengthened by the power of his love, he overcame the raging cruelty of Saul and won his persecutor on earth as his companion in heaven.... Now at last, Paul rejoices with Stephen, with Stephen he delights in the glory of Christ, with Stephen he exults, with Stephen he reigns.... This, surely, is the true life, my brothers, a life in which Paul feels no shame because of Stephen's death, and Stephen delights in Paul's companionship, for love fills them both with joy.

Which leads to the saint's closing prayer: "My brothers, Christ made love the stairway that would enable all Christians to climb to heaven. Hold fast to it, therefore, in all sincerity, give one another practical proof of it, and by your progress in it, make your ascent together."[5]

---

[5] Ibid., pp. 1256–57.

# 19

# "Converts to Rome during the XIXth Century"

William Gordon-Gorman compiled a book with the name above and published it in Britain in 1885.[1] You might think it consists of conversion stories, perhaps led by John Henry Newman and other converts from the Oxford Movement. But it is simply a directory, as the subtitle states: "A List of About Four Thousand Protestants Who Have Recently Become Roman Catholics".

It groups converts by class, university, profession, and country. "Nobility and Gentry", running fourteen pages, includes "the late William Wilberforce, sometime M.P. for Hull; eldest son of the Slave Emancipator". "Arts and Sciences" includes "John Godard, celebrated in early photography" and "Andrew Currie, the sculptor".

It might not mean much to us now, but to a British readership it would have been impressive that distinguished scholar-converts from Magdalen College, Oxford, were thirteen in number and, from Balliol, seventeen in number, including "Gerard M. Hopkins, M.A., Fellow of

---

[1] A second edition was published in London by Swan Sommenschein and Co., 1885.

the Royal University of Ireland; a Jesuit and Professor of Classics at the University College, Dublin".

That children or grandchildren became converts makes a point. From Saint John's College, Cambridge: "Professor F. A. Paley, M.A., grandson of the author of 'Evidences'; till lately Professor of Classics at the Catholic University College, Kensington, W.; Classical Examiner for the London University; author".

Likewise, wives: "Mrs. J. Curran, wife of James Curran, a Quaker, of Dublin;" "Mrs. Hoyt, wife of the Rev. W. H. Hoyt, an Episcopalian rector at Vermont;" "Mrs. Elizabeth Augustine King, wife of the late Dr. Richard King, the polar traveller". It is a good bet that the husband converts eventually if the wife does.

Near the end of the book, there is a separate "List of a Few Foreign Converts". From America:

> The late Orestes A. Brownson, LL.D., the distinguished reviewer, whom Lord Brougham styled "the master-mind of America".
> The late Stephen Douglas, statesman.
> The late Horace Greeley.
> Henry Adams Thayer, of Cambridge, Mass.

Catholicism claimed Stephen Douglas as a convert: the *Catholic Encyclopedia* calls him "a convert to Catholicism", perhaps on private knowledge, since his wife was a Catholic; he consented to have his children raised Catholic; and the bishop of Chicago presided over a Catholic burial service for him.

From "The Army and the Navy" in America, one finds: "General Joseph Warren Revere, of Boston, grandson of Paul Revere, of Revolutionary Fame, and of General Joseph Warren, who was killed at the Battle of Bunker Hill".

Among "Ladies":

Miss Allen, of Vermont, grand-daughter of General Ethan
Allen, of the Revolutionary War

Miss Harriott Prescott, well-known in American literary
circles

Rev. Mother Seton, foundress of the Sisters of Charity in
America

Mrs. Tyler, wife of Ex-President Tyler, her daughter and
granddaughter

Yes, Mother Seton was received into the Catholic Church
in the nineteenth century, on March 14, 1805. Harriott Prescott is better known by her acquired surname by
marriage, Spofford. She gained immediate fame in 1859
through a short story, "In a Cellar", published in the *At-
lantic Monthly*. It is not easy to find any of her works in
print today, but Project Gutenberg has a collection.

What is the point of such a list? The author in his pref-
ace to the second edition quotes a reviewer: the work
"gives one a startling view of the rapid advancement that
Roman Catholicism has made of late years in certain quar-
ters". The advancement is startling because it is contrary
to common expectations, the "political correctness" of the
time, which was a general "anti-popery".

Catholicism was supposed to fade away after the Ref-
ormation. It was a religion of superstition, ignorance, and
oppression. It left no room for persons of strong conviction and conscience. It was not a religion that would fit
within the bounds of reason. The remarkable develop-
ments in science, technology, and enterprise, so visible
especially in Britain and in the United States in that century, seemed out of tune with it.

And yet, here were leading figures of every walk of life
deliberately converting to Catholicism.

The book lists Newman as one of several converts from Trinity College, Oxford. But he is one among many, not the chief, not a paradigm or leader:

> Rev. John Henry Newman, D.D., M.A., Fellow of Oriel College; B.D. of this University and formerly Vicar of Saint Mary-the-Virgin, Oxford; for some time Rector of the Catholic University; now Cardinal and Superior of the Birmingham Oratory; author of hymns and of various esteemed works.[2]

After all, the Oxford Movement, a full two generations before this book, might have looked as if it were spent: those converts became Catholic priests instead of Anglican clergymen, and that was all; it was over. But the book shows, rather, that the Oxford Movement itself was part of something much more extensive.

"Second springs" seem to recur, and we might wonder when and why. There was a kind of clearing in civilization after the Enlightenment and French Revolution, and the Catholic Church did not die, but she came roaring back. Yet another spring was the great "Catholic Intellectual Renaissance" of the early twentieth century, discussed so well by Robert Royal in his book *A Deeper Vision: The Catholic Intellectual Tradition in the Twentieth Century*. Pope Leo XIII's revival of Thomism through his encyclical *Aeterni Patris* seems to have been its original impetus.

Most recently a shorter spring—or was it simply a momentary thawing?—seemed to coalesce around Father Richard J. Neuhaus, in his sympathy with Pope Saint John Paul II, in the face of a threatening culture of death.

---

[2] William Gordon-Gorman, *Converts to Rome during the XIXth Century* (London: Swan Sonnenschein and Co., 1885), 33.

But will someone be able to compile an equally impressive book, *Converts to Rome During the XXI Century*? Are we about to see another Second Spring of even greater extensiveness—as John Paul II anticipated—nourished by the blood of the millions of martyrs of the last century?

But what you and I need to ponder is this: conversions are preceded by fidelity. If we really want to see something like the historic surges in conversions, let's resolve to live our Christian calling with the intensity, faithfulness, and integrity that, through graces largely hidden, can win souls in generations to come.

# Part III

# Mary and Joseph

# 20

# Singular Vessel of Devotion

During pregnancy, some cells from the unborn child migrate through the placenta into the mother's bloodstream. These cells are "pluripotent", that is, they are capable of developing into many types of tissue. If a cell like this finds its way into breast tissue, for example, it will mimic the cells around it and develop into a breast cell, remaining there for the life of the mother.

"Mothers around the world say they feel like their children are still a part of them long after they've given birth", said a recent *Smithsonian Magazine* article. "As it turns out, that is literally true. During pregnancy, cells from the fetus cross the placenta and enter the mother's body, where they can become part of her tissues."[1]

It works the other way, too. Cells from the mother also cross the barrier. But these cells are not "pluripotent"; their lifespans and possible influences are short-lived.

Evolutionary biologists are fascinated by the exchange because they regard it as a symbiosis that contributes to the "fitness" of both mother and child. Preliminary evidence suggests that cells from her unborn child may stimulate a

---

[1] Viviane Callier, "Baby's Cells Can Manipulate Mom's Body for Decades", *Smithsonian Magazine*, September 2, 2015, https://www.smithsonianmag.com /science-nature/babys-cells-can-manipulate-moms-body-decades-180956493/.

mother's milk production, help her wounds to heal, and strengthen her immune system.

To call the system a "symbiosis" is to say that it is not some kind of mistake, an illness, or a breakdown that cells of the unborn child find their way into the mother. Biologists would say that the mother–child system has "evolved" for their mutual benefit. Philosophy, or common sense, would say that the exchange is part of God's design for childbearing.

Let us think of Mary's pregnancy in this way. Jesus was "perfect God and perfect man", like us in all ways except sin. Therefore, let us suppose that cells from the unborn Jesus migrated into Mary's blood and lodged in various organs, where they took on the functions of those organs and remained there until Mary was assumed into heaven. They were not Mary's cells, but the cells of the Lord, alive within Mary's body and playing the same function as Mary's cells. What, then, are the theological implications? (We mean, implications for us *amateurs*, that is, "lovers".)

First, that traditional Church teaching, that Jesus had no brothers and sisters, because Joseph never had relations with Mary, becomes on its own overwhelmingly convincing. To a thoughtful person, the argument from fittingness always did make sense: Why would a man go where God had been and claim for his purposes what had already been taken and reserved for divine purposes? But now Mary becomes the place where, in an important sense, God still is. It is not that, as during pregnancy, she *was* the Ark of the Covenant: it is rather that she *is* and *remains* that, since traces of the body and blood of the Lord are within her.

Second, that traditional Church teaching, that Mary was free from original sin when Jesus was conceived within her, becomes even more strongly verified. Sin and God are simply not compatible. By her carrying Jesus, God was to become in an important sense present in the very fabric of her body. That presence seems incompatible with anything in her body geared toward sin, which the presence of original sin would imply.

A point of Catholic information: the doctrine of the Immaculate Conception additionally holds that this freedom from original sin was conferred on Mary from the first moment of her existence. That she was free from original sin and its effects when she conceived Jesus was never in dispute.

The old *Catholic Encyclopedia* states well the traditional argument for this Immaculate Conception: "There is an incongruity in the supposition that the flesh, from which the flesh of the Son of God was to be formed, should ever have belonged to one who was the slave of that archenemy, whose power He came on earth to destroy."[2] The modern discovery of fetal cells that remain in the mother adds biological support to the argument.

A third implication is that Mary becomes a permanent tabernacle, literally and not just figuratively. The Litany of Loreto, after all, gives her this title: "Spiritual Vessel. Vessel of Honor. Singular Vessel of Devotion. . . . House of God. Ark of the Covenant."

Perhaps when we say these words, we think back in our imaginations to Mary as pregnant. We suppose that these words are true of her now, only because they were once true—in the way, maybe, that a former president is called "Mr. President".

True, in a pious heart, Mary's role gets attributed to her eternally because her gift of self to the Christ in her *fiat* was so complete. But it seems that here, as in other areas

---

[2] *The Catholic Encyclopedia*, ed. Charles G. Herbermann et al. (New York: Robert Appleton Company, 1910), under "Immaculate Conception".

of our faith, God is not content to leave things abstract but wishes to concretize spiritual realities. In accordance with the Incarnational Principle, the cells of the Lord that remained in Mary's body would be a permanent, concrete sign of her role as *theotokos*.

I sometimes wonder when I think of these things whether we do not do damage to Christmas by our tendency to neglect the Epiphany, which is also to neglect Mary. Epiphany is the feast of appearance and revelation. But the Lord is revealed through His Mother: she bears Him; she brings Him to light; she holds Him; she continues to present Him to us. "(And a sword will pierce through your own soul also), that thoughts out of many hearts may be revealed", Simeon said to Mary (Lk 2:35).

Mary by her maternity is a vessel of honor, but not a mere vessel, and not a vessel long ago, to be put aside after it has served a purpose, but here and now, irreducibly and still God's chosen way to approaching the Christ child with haste.

# 21

# Putting the Immaculate Conception in Christmas

On December 8, homilists are fond—and rightly so—of connecting the mystery of the Immaculate Conception with the mystery of Christmas, which is soon to come.[1] But do we forget about the Immaculate Conception when Christmas arrives, to our loss?

Curiously it was a Protestant clergyman, Phillips Brooks, who simply out of good, instinctive Christian piety wrote a hymn that celebrated the Immaculate Conception, or seemed to at least, "O Little Town of Bethlehem".

The year was 1868, only fourteen years after the dogmatic definition by Pope Pius IX in his bull *Ineffabilis Deus* that "the most Blessed Virgin Mary, in the first instance of her conception, by a singular grace and privilege granted by Almighty God, in view of the merits of Jesus Christ, the Savior of the human race, was preserved free from all stain of original sin."

Brooks was the distinguished rector at the Episcopal Church of the Holy Trinity in Philadelphia. He wrote the words of the hymn *ad hoc* for a Christmas pageant for

---

[1] The Church never disputed whether Mary was free from original sin when she conceived Jesus. Luther and Calvin did not dispute it. What was at issue, rather, was when she was cleansed from original sin. The doctrine of the Immaculate Conception is that she was so cleansed from the beginning of her existence.

children in his Sunday school. His organist looked for inspiration and composed the familiar tune at the last moment. Neither of them expected that the hymn would have any life beyond that first use. Brooks' handwritten sketch had this penultimate verse (emphasis mine):

> Where children pure and happy
> Pray to the Blessed Child,
> Where misery cries out to Thee
> *Son of the Undefiled*,
> Where Charity stands watching
> And Faith holds wide the door,
> The dark night wakes the glory hearts
> And Christmas comes once more.

Yet even by the time the pageant was performed, Brooks had changed his mind and made the fourth line "Son of the mother mild". Afterward, for the rest of his life, he wanted that this verse be omitted whenever the hymn was sung.

The *Oxford English Dictionary* shows that although the word "undefiled" had been used in earlier centuries to mean "chaste", or when applied to Mary "virginal", by the mid-1800s it meant only "without sin". The entry cites as typical a hymn from 1875 by John S.B. Monsell, "God of That Glorious Gift": "Make him and keep him Thine own child, Meek follower of the Undefiled!"—that is, a disciple of Jesus, the only sinless one, it is implied.[2]

I have known Catholics with good judgment who will not include "O Little Town of Bethlehem" in their carol-singing parties on the grounds that it is a "Unitarian hymn", celebrating Jesus solely as a "great moral teacher" and not God incarnate. I do not think that is a fair criticism, as the last line in addressing the infant Jesus as "Our

---

[2] *Oxford English Dictionary*, "undefiled", accessed September 2024, https://dio.org/10.1093/OED/8581862906.

Lord, Emmanuel"—God with us—at least admits of a trinitarian interpretation.

For decades, however, even Protestants judged the hymn inappropriate for a worship service. They omitted it from their hymnals, on the grounds that its meter and tune are that of a ballade and the words are mainly sentimental reflections rather than prayers addressed to God. I do not know the exact year when Catholics began singing it, but older hymnals certainly left it out. It seems to be regarded now as completely unobjectionable and is even included in hymnals that have high standards, like the *Adoremus Hymnal*.

That omitted phrase, however, "Son of the Undefiled", when naturally taken to affirm the Immaculate Conception, would surely have saved the whole. Why? Because the Christmas mystery like other mysteries combines opposites, which we might call in this case "the sentimental" and "the bracing".

Sentimental would be shepherd boys with pan pipes, oxen and donkeys, candlelight, the romanticism of a cave, wondrous guests showing up from afar, and angels as we like to imagine them—as in many of John Rutter's very endearing carols.

Bracing would be angels as they actually appear, the emperor's command of a census, the market fact of a housing shortage, Herod's henchmen, and all intimations of the Passion. (*Nota bene*: Mary's birth pangs are not among them, since she did not suffer any.)

Philosophically, what is sentimental is soft, fuzzy, and blends from one thing to another, while what is bracing is hard and has sharp boundaries.

Where does Mary fall in this? Should she be reckoned as on the mild side of the mystery, solely, or on the bracing side as well? Or put the question this way: Because of Mary's role, must not the mystery of Christmas also be carried over to Mary and include her? But what about Mary could be "bracing" after all?

As to Mary's role: she is the throne at Christmas. Yes, paintings depict pious shepherds kneeling with Joseph and Mary around a manger in adoration. But in reality, visitors never come to see a baby, but the mother with her baby. They stay away from sleeping babies, as a rule, and approach the baby only when he is in his mother's arms.

For children, who are perhaps the most sentimental (and most bracing) among us, especially is this true, as Chateaubriand puts it marvelously in his *Genius of Christianity*: "Mary is the refuge of innocence, of weakness, and of misfortune.... The mother carries her babe before Mary's image, and this little one, though it knows not as yet the God of Heaven, already knows this holy mother (*cette divine mère*) who holds an infant in her arms."[3]

It is the Immaculate Conception that makes Mary bracing because it marks a discontinuity, the sharp initiation of a new creation. It is the same discontinuity as that of sin versus forgiveness, of being unbaptized versus being baptized, of "men of goodwill" versus "men on whom his favor rests"—as that between a great moral teacher and a Savior. Is Mary mild, or undefiled?

Brooks' hymn is slushy without the Immaculate Conception. It is a hymn of "insofar as": insofar as we open our hearts, the dear Christ enters in, etc. Of course, Christmas is designed, not to repel anyone, but to welcome all comers insofar as they want to approach.

But "Do not destroy the mystery!"—as Saint Thomas Aquinas would say. Put the God-Man, and the Immaculate Conception, in Christmas.

---

[3] François-Renée Chateaubriand and Charles Ignatius White, *The Genius of Christianity; or, the Spirit and Beauty of the Christian Religion*, 15th rev. ed. (Baltimore: John Murphy, 1856), p. 67.

## 22

# A Shout-Out to Mary

I had always pictured the Visitation as an intimate affair. Paintings display it in that way also: two holy women, perhaps embracing, sharing in confidence the great things that God was accomplishing in them through the children they bore in their wombs. What is more intimate than pregnancy?

So maybe you are sometimes brought up short, as was I, by Luke's language of "exclaimed with a loud cry":

> When Elizabeth heard the greeting of Mary, the child leaped in her womb; and Elizabeth was filled with the Holy Spirit and she exclaimed with a loud cry, "Blessed are you among women, and blessed is the fruit of your womb! And why is this granted me, that the mother of my Lord should come to me? For behold, when the voice of your greeting came to my ears, the child in my womb leaped for joy. And blessed is she who believed that there would be a fulfilment of what was spoken to her from the Lord." (Lk 1:41–45)

If anything, the phrase is under-translated. The Greek verb (*anaphōneō*) means strictly to shout aloud, even, to make a great noise, as in this verse where it is used in the Greek

Septuagint: "So all Israel brought up the ark of the covenant of the LORD with shouting, and with the sound of the horn, with trumpets, *with the loud-sounding of cymbals*, with harps, and lyres" (1 Chron 15:28, emphasis added).

Imagine now Elizabeth first banging a cymbal to get attention and then shouting out commensurately. That in effect is what Luke is depicting.

The language "in a loud voice" is just as striking. Again, this language is an under-translation. The Greek noun means strictly a shout, or even a piercing wail. Jesus uses the word for the proclamation of the bridegroom's arrival: "At midnight *there was a cry*, 'Behold, the bridegroom! Come out to meet him'" (Mt 25:6, emphasis added). John uses the word to mean a clamor of distress (Rev 21:4).

This kind of shouting of Elizabeth, as if making a public proclamation to a crowd, is said to be the effect of the Holy Spirit filling her and also, apparently, of the leaping of the infant in her womb. That infant, of course, was the Baptist, the one whose voice, also in the Spirit, would later be shouting in the wilderness (Mk 1:3). John leaps when Elizabeth hears the voice of Mary, and Elizabeth shouts when John leaps. Elizabeth seems to be both the ears and the voice of her son.

The commentators are generally silent on this "crying out in a loud voice" or say foolish things ("an unrestrained utterance under the influence of irrepressible feeling, thoroughly true to feminine nature", says one).[1] But Saint Ambrose gets it: *Magna voce clamavit, ubi domini sensit adventum.* "She shouted out loudly when she realized the Lord had come."[2]

---

[1] William Robertson Nicoll, *The Expositor's Greek Testament* (London: Hodder and Stoughton, 1897).

[2] *Catena Aurea*, trans. John Henry Newman, vol. 3, pt. 1 (1841), chap. 1.

After I realized what was going on in this verse, I thought of the prayer, the Hail Mary.[3] Apparently, that prayer did not take the form we use today until around 1500. In that form, it has traditionally been described as having four parts: the first part was contributed by an angel (Lk 1:28); the second, by Elizabeth (v. 42 in the above); the third, the holy name of Jesus, by the popes; the fourth, the closing petition, by the piety of the faithful.

Surely the second part, "Blessed art thou among women", etc.—words inspired by the Holy Spirit, given apparently through a prophet (the Baptist), and even shouted aloud by Elizabeth in the presence of the Lord—surely words delivered in this way, in this context, are not just mere curiosities for Christians henceforth, but something like a canon of prayer. How could the Protestant Reformers, for instance, (some of them) have scrupled at this prayer?

Looking at the verses anew, I was also called up short by the parallelism:

blessed are you among women
blessed is the fruit of your womb

The same Greek word is used for "blessed" in each case. Read the clauses in the less familiar, opposite order, and it becomes striking that Mary is called blessed in exactly the same way the Holy One, the Lord, is called blessed. To be sure, her blessedness comes from the blessedness of the Lord. We must assert this. Of course, she is a creature, not a fit object of adoration or *latria*. Nonetheless, at least as far as Elizabeth's shouted words are concerned, the honors,

---

[3] Hail Mary, full of grace, the Lord is with thee. Blessed art thou among women, and blessed is the fruit of thy womb, Jesus. Holy Mary, Mother of God, pray for us sinners, now and at the hour of our death. Amen.

the standing, the reverence due, the cause for joy are all the same. (The tradition marks out this attitude of reverence with a special name, *hyperdulia*.)

In his *Harmony* of the Gospels, even John Calvin, after being worried by the language—"She seems to put Mary and Christ on an equal footing, which would have been highly improper"—admits: "At this day the blessedness brought us by Christ cannot be the subject of our praise, without reminding us, at the same time, of the distinguished honor which God was pleased to bestow upon Mary."[4]

But Calvin also said some foolish things about the Hail Mary. The first part, he said, involved taking the angel's words for our own, which (to him) was impertinent. And it used that greeting to address what he considered an absent person, which in his view was foolish. "With extraordinary ignorance have the Papists, by an enchanter's trick, changed this salutation into a prayer."[5]

I will close this essay by letting Major Julian Cook refute Calvin. Crossing the river Waal during Operation Market Garden on September 17, 1944, Cook rallied the men to row evenly using only a fragment of the angel's greeting, as Cornelius Ryan reported in *A Bridge Too Far*: "'The Lord is with thee' was too long," Cook later said, "so I kept repeating, 'Hail Mary,' (one stroke), 'Full of grace' (second stroke)." And so on.[6]

Major Cook, too, cried out in a loud voice. And no one doubted he was saying a prayer.

---

[4] Jean Calvin, *Commentary on a Harmony of the Evangelists, Matthew, Mark and Luke* (Grand Rapids: W.B. Eerdmans, 1956), p. 49.

[5] Ibid., p. 33.

[6] Robert Redford plays Cook in the scene, in the 1977 film of *A Bridge Too Far*.

## 23

# In Honor of Mary

In honor of the Immaculate Conception and Our Lady of Guadalupe,[1] I invite you to ponder with me the two opening lines of Mary's song, the "Magnificat" (Lk 1:46–47).

We are confronted first with the fact that Mary even composed a song. She must indeed have composed it in advance and memorized it, repeating it to Luke later. Did she do so out of obedience to what is found in the prophet Isaiah? Consider some verses in Isaiah 12:

> 1 You will say in that day:
> "I will give thanks to you, O LORD,
> 2 for the LORD GOD is my strength and my song,
>   and he has become my salvation."
> 3 With joy you will draw water from the wells of
>   salvation.
> 4 And you will say in that day:
> "Give thanks to the LORD,
> call upon his name;
> make known his deeds among the nations,
> proclaim that his name is exalted." ...
> 6 "Shout, and sing for joy ... for great in your
>   midst is the Holy One of Israel."

[1] First published in *The Boston Pilot*, December 8, 2023.

It would take someone who loved Scripture very much to read such words and then to aim to fulfill them, by literally composing a song on the stated theme—and then by memorizing the song, and taking care to pass it on, so as to "make known his deeds among the nations", as has surely happened.

We can presume that Elizabeth was of the same mind, and so we see Mary forming with her a little "Benedict community", so to speak, of women who foster and share among themselves, and are aware that they are doing so, a deep love for their inheritance in Israel.

Mary's song has been set to music by Taverner, Tallis, Palestrina, Guerrero, Lassus, Byrd, Victoria, Monteverdi, Gibbons, Schutz, Charpentier, Pachelbel, Purcell, Vivaldi, Telemann, J. S. Bach (and two of his sons besides), Mozart, Schubert, Mendelssohn, Liszt, Bruckner, Tchaikovsky, Vaughn Williams, Rachmaninoff, and Rutter—among others.

If imitation is the sincerest form of flattery, then the entire civilization of music praises Mary. Catholic attempts to honor her through what is called "hyperdulia" almost fall short in comparison with the adornments brought to her by music. The Muses have ceded their place to the Virgin.

"In the early 12th century, the Virgin had been the supreme protectress of civilisation. She had taught a race of tough and ruthless barbarians the virtues of tenderness and compassion. The great cathedrals of the Middle Ages were her dwelling places upon earth" is the testimony of Kenneth Clark in his series, "Civilization".[2]

So we are confronted at the start by someone who loves Scripture, ponders it, assesses her life in relation to it, and

---

[2] Kenneth Clark, *Civilization*, episode 7, "Grandeur and Experience". See Kenneth Clark and British Broadcasting Corporation, *Civilisation: A Personal View* (London: British Broadcasting Corp., 1969), p. 129.

then makes sacrifices to be obedient to it. Her great love for Scripture resulted in her very words becoming enshrined in Scripture. The Holy Spirit took her words for his own. Thus, God honors her before we honor her.

Of this line, "My soul doth magnify the Lord," observe that it takes for granted that already *in her body* she is "magnifying the Lord", in the sense that he is growing within her, taking his flesh from her flesh. If we had a silhouette of expecting Mary, we could point to it and say: Her magnified body doth magnify the Lord.

But as regards her soul, I find that nothing surpasses what Origen wrote:

> Now if the Lord could neither receive increase or decrease, what is this that Mary speaks of, My soul doth magnify the Lord? But if I consider that the Lord our Savior is the image of the invisible God, and that the soul is created according to His image, so as to be an image of an image, then I shall see plainly, that as after the manner of those who are accustomed to paint images, each one of us forming his soul after the image of Christ, makes it great or little, base or noble, after the likeness of the original so when I have made my soul great in thought, word, and deed, the image of God is made great, and the Lord Himself whose image it is, is magnified in my soul.[3]

Here we find two profound thoughts. The first is that Mary's role is akin to the Incarnation, in that she images the image who images the Father. She does so by God's choice, not her own.

The second is that she could not have said these words truly, and they are true ("Your word is truth", Jn 17:17, "Scripture cannot be nullified", Jn 10:35), unless she was "great" already in "thought, word, and deed". Let us admit

[3] *Catena Aurea*, vol. 3, pt. 1, chap. 1.

that it is startling for someone to say that in his soul he has made the Lord appear even greater than He is. Such a statement must be an expression of either the greatest humility or utter madness. But, again, Scripture is true.

Mary goes on to say, "My spirit rejoices in God my Savior." Saint Basil rightly sees that the Greek word for "rejoices" points back to the Baptist leaping for joy in Elizabeth's womb. He comments, "Because then the holy Virgin had drunk in all the graces of the Spirit, she rightly adds, And my spirit has leaped for joy."[4]

But note that she refers to God immediately as "my" Savior, not "the" Savior. She was free from sin from the moment of her conception, we confess, but because God was her Savior in particular.

[4] Ibid.

## 24

# God's Instrument for Viewing the Crucifixion

The Crucifixion is so horrible that we naturally recoil from it. Without some special reason to view it, we flee from it, just as the Apostles did at the event itself (except for John). Protest as much as we like that we are ready to die with Him, our nature rebels, and we flee.

Our Protestant brethren prove that this is so. They understand that they must show piety toward the act that saved them. But perhaps because they reject "this is my body" in the literal sense, they have no strong reason to re-imagine the corpus. Thus, they erect crosses only. They wear only crosses as pendants, never crucifixes.

The Catholic devotion of Stations of the Cross can be understood in this light. To go to a church for the Stations is to bind ourselves, against our inclinations, to follow the distressing torture all the way to the end. We imitate Odysseus binding himself to the mast, but in this case, to keep us from avoiding rather than pursuing.

According to tradition, Mary devised the stations in the yard of the household in Ephesus, where she lived with John. Pause and consider how astonishing this fact is. I have known mothers who have lost children. They save locks of hair and pictures. They remember times together.

But they do not try to re-enact, on a regular basis, the last moments of their child's death.

But this was the woman who "kept all these things, pondering them in her heart" (Lk 2:19), who, by the prophecy of Simeon, was told that "a sword will pierce through your own soul also that thoughts out of many hearts may be revealed" (2:35). If she paid at least as much attention to these words as we do, she must have understood that her special vocation was to contemplate and, by contemplating, to bring to us the Crucifixion of her Son.

Apparently, she acted on this understanding. She did so by devising the stations. And we help her fulfill this vocation when we follow the Stations ourselves.

Catholics say that Mary is a mediatrix of the redemption. Some take umbrage at this. They say: "Do not place anything between us and the Lord." But suppose that, practically speaking, we would not "get" to the Lord if we did not have some bridge, some connector, some means—someone to draw us, someone to lead us in, someone (even) to buffer. Then humility would require that we plead, rather: "Please give us this mediatrix, so that we can (after all) get to the Lord as we wish!"

This is the spirit in which, I think, we should understand that ancient hymn called after its first Latin words, "*Stabat mater*" ("The mother was standing"). In the hymn, we see the Crucifixion precisely through its effects on Mary. Look carefully at its lyrics, and you will see that the hymn never asks us to look at the Crucifixion itself. She is standing there next to the Cross, in tears. A sword pierces her through while she looks upon the punishments her glorious Son endures. She sees how Jesus has endured a terrible scourging. She sees "her sweet offspring, abandoned in death, as he gives up his spirit". But we never see any of this: we see her seeing it.

In Catholic tradition, the Son is likened to the sun, and Mary to the moon. We look upon Mary in the way that we look at the sun in a reflection. And then, when the Son dies, the sun dies—"darkness over the whole land" (Lk 23:44)—so that it remains for us only to ponder the divinely appointed reflectrix, who "stood at a distance".

If we are slow to feel passion at the Passion, Mary can help us. "How sad and afflicted that blessed woman was!" the hymn says, "Who is the man who is incapable of weeping, upon seeing the very Mother of Christ immersed so deeply in suffering? Who can fail to feel sorrow along with her, when he contemplates the pain that the Mother of Christ shares with her Son?" Mary strangely attracts us to the pain. She binds us to His suffering.

Protestant critics of Marian devotion say that Catholics worship Mary. Really? Attend to the petitions at the end of this great hymn:

- "Mother, fountain of love, make me feel the power of your sorrow, that I might mourn with you!
- "Holy Mother, this is my request: fix firmly in my heart the wounds of the Crucified One!
- "Divide up with me the punishments of your wounded Son, who deigned to suffer for me!
- "Make me weep piously along with you. Make me, like you, suffer with him on the Cross, for as long as I shall live!
- "This I desire: that through my own grieving I might stand next to the Cross keeping company with you!
- "Make it so that I become injured by his wounds; make it so that I become drunk by the Cross and by the blood of your Son!"

The Latin of the *Stabat Mater* is so beautiful that someone might reasonably wish to learn Latin simply to read it. The hymn has been graced by two musical settings that rank as great masterpieces: those of Palestrina and Pergolesi.

Not a movie, but Mary is God's instrument for viewing the Crucifixion.

## 25

# Here Comes That Dreamer!

We study the Christmas story in part because we are supposed to imitate its good actors and avoid the sins of the bad actors. Or call it the Christmas "history" rather than "story", because it really happened, and God uses realities to signify truths, as we use symbols. Sacred history is His story. We are meant to learn lessons of the past and repeat them.

Consider Joseph in this history. We praise him for his prudence. You may know the traditional prayer, *Fecit eum Deus quasi patrem regis*—"God made him as it were the father of the King and steward over his whole household."

The prayer hearkens back to Joseph, son of Jacob, in Egypt. We know so little of Mary's husband that pious tradition rightly tells us to look to that earlier Joseph as an image and type. The Church licenses our imaginations to think of the Galilean carpenter's life as informed, more fully, by realities discoverable in that Prince of Egypt.

You want to know what the secret life of Jesus was like in the humble home of Nazareth? Pharaoh's court will give you an idea.

Christmas history tells us that Saint Joseph was thoughtful. He proceeded with what lawyers call "due diligence". Matthew portrays him as carefully considering what he ought to do after he found that Mary had conceived by the Holy Spirit.

Yet although he was careful, he was also decisive. When the angel next tells him to take Mary as his wife, he immediately rises from sleep and does it. There is no delay, no hesitation. Apparently Mary, who said *fiat* so resolutely, was matched with a partner who showed a corresponding, manly definiteness of will.

Likewise, when the angel tells him to take the Holy Family to Egypt, Matthew describes this as: immediately Joseph gets up from sleep, they leave. In the tradition, one finds speculation that gold from the magi, providentially, made advance planning for such a trip dispensable.

To Joseph is given the important legal role of naming the child: "She will bear a son, but you will give him his name." As fathers do generally, he navigated the family through the demands of legal relationships and authorities. No doubt it was Joseph who insisted that pregnant Mary accompany him to Bethlehem, to follow the emperor's decree.

So all the traditional traits of Joseph are found right there: prudent deliberation, decisive action, and complete virtue under law—which is deemed "righteousness".

Yet this list of his distinctive traits is incomplete. To see why, consider this test. Suppose you asked one hundred Catholics whether they thought it essential to be open to messages from God in dreams, how many would say, "Of course"? And yet this was essential for Jesus to live beyond infancy.

Consider how natural agents were moving then to reach a certain outcome. Herod pretended to want to worship the "King of the Jews" but intended to murder the child. The Holy Family was apparently settled in Bethlehem and had no reason for leaving. The magi were going to pay a friendly return visit to Herod's court on the road back to their home countries.

The result of all of these "natural causes" was predictably the death of the child. He was waiting there vulnerable, in a crib in Bethlehem: easy to find and easy to execute. Without question, Herod, with his spies, would be able to track Him down and destroy Him.

It was only an attention to dreams that prevented this outcome: the magi heeded a warning they received in a dream, and Joseph immediately carried out a message he learned in a dream. We think we need to imitate the good actors in the Christmas story. But do we imitate their attention to dreams? How would we do so?

Almost no one reads the part of the *Summa Theologiae* that follows the treatise on the virtues, "Of Acts Which Pertain Especially to Certain Men". It covers prophecy, vision, and dreams, among other things. Apparently Saint Thomas thought such matters an important auxiliary to virtue.

Speaking surely as one who knows, the Angelic Doctor remarks that "the abstraction from the senses takes place in the prophets without any subversion of the order of nature; it is due to some well-ordered cause, which may be natural, as for instance, sleep, or by the intensity of contemplation."[1] His general teaching is that visions follow upon fervent striving in prayer.

The early Church Fathers held something similar about the magi in particular. They came to worship God incarnate and desired deeply to learn from Him. Perhaps they were even expecting the infant to speak to them. He did not, as this would have revealed His divinity too early. However, they were granted a compensatory privilege.

Strikingly, in Joseph's dreams, Matthew always says it is an "angel of the Lord" who addresses him. But of the magi, Matthew says simply that their message is from God.

[1] *Summa Theologica* II-II, q. 173, a. 3, corpus.

Always attentive to such details, Saint Jerome comments, "They had offered gifts to the Lord and receive a warning corresponding to it. This warning, which 'they received as a response,' is given, not by an angel, but by the Lord Himself, to shew the high privilege granted to the merit of Joseph."[2] Saint Jerome like other Fathers apparently assigned a comparable role to both Mary and Joseph at the side of the infant Christ. "Life returned by the same entrance through which death had entered in", Saint Remigius teaches. "By Adam's disobedience we were ruined, by Joseph's obedience we all begin to be recalled to our former condition."[3] His obedience to visions found fruit even in the truthful visions of others.

To follow Saint Joseph, then, at Christmas: Bring your concerns to prayer. Work through them manfully in God's presence. But implore His advice. And, if you receive intimations and inspirations, act on them boldly.

Expect that the best way to live is prudently, but also with divine assistance.

---

[2] *Catena Aurea*, trans. John Henry Newman, vol. 1, pt. 1 (1841), chap. 2.
[3] Ibid., p. 57.

# 26

# Doing Justice to Saint Joseph—I

As we are beginning the Year of Saint Joseph,[1] and Christmas is near, consider with me the role of Saint Joseph in the Annunciation. This verse in particular: "Her husband Joseph, being a just man and unwilling to put her to shame, resolved to send her away quietly" (Mt 1:19). If you attended Mass last Friday, you heard this verse in the Gospel. And perhaps like me, you heard a homily that gave a common interpretation of this verse.

That common interpretation begins by assuming that Joseph believed Mary had had relations with another man. It is natural to assume this. But is it really true? This is the premise I wish to challenge.

The common interpretation continues as follows: A betrothal was a formal contract similar to marriage. Infidelity during betrothal was equivalent to adultery. As Joseph was a "just man", he did not wish to take into his home an adulterer—an unrepentant adulterer, since Mary had in no way admitted her infidelity. Or asked his forgiveness.

As he was the merciful sort of righteous man, he did not want to see her punished or humiliated or even possibly stoned. Therefore, he decided to divorce her discreetly, rather than make a big public display of it, as was his option.

---

[1] Published December 22, 2020.

This common interpretation was favored by Saint John Chrysostom and appears in the notes to the New American Bible. But is it true?

If so, first, why would Matthew have taken care to stipulate that "Mary was found with child through the Holy Spirit"? If he is telling the story from Joseph's point of view, why would he not tell this crucial detail, too, from Joseph's point of view, say, "Joseph was downcast to find that she was with child"?

Second, why would the angel have begun, "Do not be afraid to take Mary your wife into your home"? Fear had nothing to do with Joseph's decision, on the common interpretation. Moreover, on that interpretation, please note, Joseph would not be "suspecting" or "fearing that" Mary had committed adultery—he would be absolutely certain of it!

Third, Joseph had moral certainty of Mary's virtue, and there were no grounds to believe that infidelity was possible. Even decent Christians today, wholesome, good-intentioned, sometimes find that they know each other's character so well as to be certain that infidelity is excluded. Joseph and Mary were like this always. Then Mary had no faults, which in an innocent person are necessary preparations or preconditions of adultery. She did not drink to excess or flirt. She was not susceptible to seduction from need of affirmation or praise.

She would not even be alone with another man. Her relationship to Joseph itself had no "drives" toward sexual immorality. They had compacted not even to have relations after marriage. Add that Nazareth was a small town of a dozen tiny stone houses on a hill. (I have seen the excavation.) Few things happen in such a place unobserved.

Fourth, to the extent that we love, we trust, and we are obliged to trust. It can be a serious sin to suspect sin in someone whom we have come to love over time on good grounds. If a husband out of jealousy reads something disreputable into his wife's innocent behavior, he sins against her. If Joseph had believed Mary guilty of gross infidelity, he would have sinned against her and needed to ask her forgiveness before taking her as his wife.

"But she was with child!"—you will say—"surely that is evidence." Not necessarily. Innocent people do not think of sex and pregnancy in this way. Joseph was shown no anatomical charts in health class. He had no "experience with women". To an innocent person, there is no necessary connection between pregnancy and sex; it was possible for him to hold these apart.

Fifth, surely Saint Joseph had at least as much faith as other saints. God told Abraham to sacrifice Isaac, while He also told Abraham that through Isaac he would be the father of many nations. Saint Paul praises Abraham's faith precisely in holding these two truths together. Abraham's faith is even a paradigm for Christians. "Mary is innocent. Mary is with child." Can we credit Joseph with at least as much faith as Abraham? Would God have passed over the opportunity to give Joseph this particular test? Surely this was the "contradiction" that was troubling Joseph, not "Mary was innocent. Mary is no longer innocent."

Then, too, Saint Paul praises Abraham for how he resolved the contradiction, reasoning that God must be planning to raise Isaac from the dead (Heb 11:19)—as it were, discovering the doctrine of the Resurrection.

Which leads to the sixth consideration: Joseph surely knew Scripture at least as well as others, and the prophecy that (in the interpretation of the Septuagint) "a virgin will conceive and bear a son" (Is 7:14). In a time of widespread expectation of the Messiah, would Joseph be unfamiliar with this prophecy? Is it an accident that the angel's words to Joseph track this prophecy exactly? Would it have been incredible for him to suppose that Mary—Mary!—was that virgin?

If he had reached that conclusion, as he was a righteous man and therefore humble, would he not have been afraid, out of humility, to presume to join himself to her as husband, absent divine warrant?

Saint Jerome adopts this other interpretation: "This may be considered a testimony to Mary, that Joseph, confident in her purity, and wondering at what had happened, covered in silence that mystery which he could not explain."[2] Also Rabanus: "He beheld her to be with child, whom he knew to be chaste; and because he had read, 'Behold, a virgin shall conceive,' he did not doubt that this prophecy should be fulfilled in her."[3] "He sought to put her away", says Origen, "because he saw in her a great sacrament, to approach which he thought himself unworthy."[4]

Just a few reflections with which to begin the Year of the remarkable Saint Joseph.

---

[2] *Catena Aurea*, trans. John Henry Newman, vol. 1, pt. 1 (1841), chap. 2.
[3] Ibid.
[4] Ibid.

# 27

# Doing Justice to Saint Joseph—II

As a Catholic, I believe that "*sola scriptura*" is wrong. Scripture is not sufficient by itself as a rule of Christian faith. It is obviously wrong, too, because Scripture cannot say what counts as Scripture or not. So the Church is necessary, too.

But perhaps you have tended to think of this matter along these lines: there are many things we need to believe as Christians, which are only implicit, or not even clearly stated, in Scripture. Baptism is the crucial sacrament of salvation. But infant baptism is taught only implicitly: babies presumably were baptized when households were (see Acts 10:48). As for the foundational doctrine of the Trinity: it is simply not clearly stated in Scripture, or even in the early Fathers, as Newman never tired of pointing out. That is why the Council of Nicaea was necessary.

On this view, the Church is necessary as adding something that Scripture does not explicitly or clearly say.

But what if, in what it does say, Scripture sometimes looks misleading? Not that it is inherently misleading, but that we are prone to misunderstand it. What if, without the Church, people who relied on Scripture alone would go astray?

Without doubt, the narrative of the birth of Jesus is like this. Scripture on its own would lead us to think that Saint

Joseph had relations with Mary after the birth of Jesus, and even that Jesus had brothers born of Mary:

—with its language of "first-born son" (so there were others then?, Lk 2:7);
—"before they came together" (so they came together?, Mt 1:18);
—"he knew her not until she had borne a son" (then he knew her after?, Mt 1:25);
—and "brethren" of Jesus (Jn 7:3).

But the Church teaches clearly that this is not so. The *Catechism* echoes the teaching of centuries, that Mary is "ever-virgin": "Mary 'remained a virgin in conceiving her Son, a virgin in giving birth to him, a virgin in carrying him, a virgin in nursing him at her breast, always a virgin'" (citing Saint Augustine).[1] Joseph had no relations with her, and they had no other children. This truth is not up for grabs.

Not that the Church's teaching just hangs there, unsupported. Many converging lines of reasoning lead to that result.

For example, that Jesus is the only son of Mary is designed in God's Providence to mirror the fact that He is the only-begotten Son of God. You fathers and mothers who are reading this know how different the Holy Family would be if Jesus were one among many—and Joseph and Mary, like all good parents, had to raise Him without showing special preference. In that case, He could not possibly have a status, in His humanity, that represents His status in His divinity.

Or consider that Mary's womb is rightly regarded as a "shrine" and has been called such by countless holy men

---

[1] *Catechism of the Catholic Church*, no. 510.

and women. You will grant, I take it, that Mary's womb is at least as holy and consecrated to God as a tabernacle. But what decent Catholic would ever contemplate taking a tabernacle from the altar and using it for his own purposes. We cannot even say what we would have to think in this regard.

And why would Joseph and Mary want to have relations anyway? They were already, in their nuptial promises and shared love of God, as united in love as anyone can be. Through her body, Mary was espoused to the Holy Spirit. It is not as though it was for Joseph to claim or possess it. And why would they want more children to raise beyond Jesus? This would seem thoughtless and ungrateful. (Remember that children were the motive for sexual relations in traditional Jewish culture.)

As for Joseph—why would he claim Mary's virginity for himself, so to speak, when even God did not do so? Understand that it is also Church teaching that Jesus was born without passing through the birth canal and destroying Mary's physical integrity: those movies of Mary in painful labor are false.

On this question of Joseph's attitude, Aquinas in the *Summa* can hardly restrain himself. Chesterton has a fine passage in his biography of Aquinas where he contrasts Aquinas with Luther. Aquinas, he says, unlike Luther, never tried to bully someone into agreeing with him by throwing his personality around:

[Luther] was the first man who ever consciously used his consciousness or what was later called his Personality. He had as a fact a rather strong personality. Aquinas had an even stronger personality; he had a massive and magnetic presence; he had an intellect that could act like a huge system of artillery spread over the whole world; he had that

instantaneous presence of mind in debate, which alone
really deserves the name of wit. But it never occurred to
him to use anything except his wits, in defense of a truth
distinct from himself. It never occurred to Aquinas to use
Aquinas as a weapon.[2]

And yet, for all that, Aquinas sometimes becomes roused
in spirit. When it comes to the question of whether Saint
Joseph had relations with Mary, he bursts out: it would be
tantamount to an imputation of extreme presumption in
Joseph to assume that he attempted to violate her whom
by the angel's revelation he knew to have conceived by
the Holy Ghost.[3]

And this, too, makes much sense. Consider, as a remote
analogy, how a man still innocent feels a reverent fear for
his wife's natural chastity on his wedding night. And yet
the Holy Spirit is God.

But then how do we resolve those Scripture verses that
seem to say the contrary? The Church has been explaining
the apparent conflict since Saint Jerome's reply to Helvi-
dius in A.D. 383. And if you rely on "Scripture alone" in
this matter, as in others, you are liable to go not simply
wrong, but gravely wrong.

[2] G. K. Chesterton, *St. Thomas Aquinas* (New York: Sheed & Ward, 1933),
p. 245.
[3] *Summa Theologica* III, q. 28, art. 3.

# 28

# Further Justice to Saint Joseph

In this year of Saint Joseph,[1] let's at least do justice to Saint Joseph. Mere justice is the starting point of love and devotion.

In some earlier columns, I argued that we do not do justice to Saint Joseph if we take him to have doubted Mary's fidelity. We certainly do not do justice to him either if we think that he had relations with her after Our Lord's birth.

So in this column, I want to challenge the assumption that it is enough to call him a "foster father".

We often refer to Saint Joseph as the "foster father" or "guardian" of Our Lord. Echoing Scripture, we maybe even say that he was "reputed" to have been Jesus' father. Many saints and popes have used similar expressions, which are true, so far as they go. But they fail to get at the fullness of Saint Joseph's paternity.

As a father myself of a large family, this is a matter close to my heart. I address Saint Joseph in prayer as "my father", and I take him to be an example of fatherhood for myself. But could he have been in some sense "less" of a father than I am? (I mean "as father". Clearly in virtue he is stupendously greater.) Can a student be greater than his teacher? These are shocking ideas and must be false.

---

[1] Published March 2, 2021.

I find that to grapple with this question well, you need to turn to an earlier generation in the Church, when families were intact and biological paternity was taken more seriously. By contrast, we are disposed to agree too quickly that adoptive fatherhood exhausts fatherhood. In part, this is because the authority of fatherhood is being attacked across the board, especially the authority of God as Creator. Also, people do not want to appear to be criticizing broken families, where children are not raised by their biological mother and father together. We have partly good motives, too, insofar as we want to insist that raising a child is as important as engendering it.

Whatever the reasons, we too quickly accept that it is enough to call Saint Joseph a "foster father". Yet an earlier generation was unhappy with this title. I began to understand this truth reading a marvelous devotional book by a French Dominican, Michel Gasnier, *Joseph the Silent*. First published in 1960 in Paris as *Trente Visites à Joseph le Silencieux*, it was translated into English two years later.[2]

"The style of the book", wrote a contemporary reviewer, "is luminous and eloquent, as one would expect from an author whose works have been crowned by the French Academy and from a speaker whose eloquence has brought him invitations to preach in pulpits throughout France as well as in foreign countries." Scepter Press has brought out this difficult-to-find book in a new translation for the Year of Saint Joseph.

In his chapter on "Joseph's Fatherhood", Father Gasnier quotes Bossuet, who adapted a maxim from Saint John Chrysostom: "God gave Joseph all that belongs to a father without loss of virginity."[3] He refers to a congress held at the Oratory of Saint Joseph in Montreal, Canada, August 1–9, 1955, which enthusiastically adopted the expression "virginal father" to refer to Saint Joseph. Indeed, such is the invocation at the start of a popular Prayer of Consecration to Saint Joseph: "O Glorious Patriarch and Patron of the Church! O Virgin Spouse of the Virgin Mother of God! O Guardian and Virginal Father of the Word Incarnate!"[4]

Father Gasnier maintains that "virginal father" is the better expression. "It is not easy to qualify Joseph's paternity with precision," he writes, "because it represents, if one may so express it, a paternity utterly unique in history; something so special, so original as to demand a new vocabulary capable of attributing a proper title to its function."[5]

What are Father Gasnier's arguments? He points out that an adopted child is originally a stranger to at least one adoptive parent and possibly a ward of the state. But "from the moment he became incarnate in Mary, lawfully and divinely fruitful, he belonged at the same time to Joseph, since husband and wife, according to the order established by God are one, and hold their goods in common."

It is no small matter to insist that Joseph and Mary were truly "espoused" (Douay-Rheims) when she conceived, and not merely "engaged", as some paraphrase translations put it (Mt 1:18).

Joseph moreover had an active role in Jesus' conception, because of his love for Mary's virginity: "The Man-God was the fruit of Mary's virginity.... And Joseph, reverencing that virginity, prepared the way as it were for the Holy Spirit to make possible her miraculous fecundity.... Both, by common consent, had offered it to heaven as an

[4] Ibid.
[5] Ibid.

acceptable gift. And both in return had received in equal measure a son, the fruit as it were, of their virginal union." Then, too, God "transferred his rights" as Father to Joseph, as signified in the angel's words that Joseph would give the child his name, as if to say, "To you, God transmits His rights.... You will have a truly fatherly love for Him, and you will exercise all the rights of a father over Him."

Joseph was even the father of the Redeemer "by blood", because the blood that really counts in this regard is that of the mature man who offered himself on the Cross, and yet "Jesus will eat the bread earned by Joseph's toil.... It is by means of the food bought with the price of Joseph's toil that Jesus' veins will be filled with that Precious Blood which he will spill to the last drop on Calvary." Joseph's sweat becomes the Lord's blood.

Who could possibly be a better witness in this matter than Mary? In a moment of distress, she speaks of Joseph's paternity as equal to her own maternity: "Behold," she says, "your father and I have been looking for you anxiously" (Lk 2:48).

# Two Reflections on Saint Joseph

Something very characteristic of sons is that, when they like something in their fathers, they say to themselves specifically that they want to do something similar someday.

It happens all the time, in matters large and small. Once I took my children on the Skyline Drive to see the fall foliage in an old Mercedes station wagon with a sunroof. At a rest stop, from a scenic overlook, a warm breeze gently blowing, my eldest looked around at the brilliant colors, simply pleased, and he exclaimed, "When I grow up, I am going to take my children on the Skyline Drive!"

Just yesterday, my son—a senior in high school—could not start his car. I said, "Try turning the wheel." He turned it, and the car started. Astounded, he said out loud, "So this is one of those things you know because someone tells you. When I have a son, and he cannot start his car, I am going to tell him to try turning the wheel."

These are charming stories that I remember because my sons spoke their thoughts aloud. But sons have many thoughts like that unspoken, and many intimations not even voiced within.

The question then arises: Among the things that Jesus said or did, are there any that, we might suppose, He deliberately did, intending to do what Joseph had done? If so, then in doing so He was reflecting Saint Joseph.

We know that Jesus thought of His relationship to His heavenly Father in that way. He said that He did nothing except what He saw His heavenly Father do (Jn 5:19). So this was a mark of the Lord's human personality. It is obvious, too, that in His carpentry work, at least, Jesus would have been following Joseph.

We might make something of a challenge out of it for the Year of Saint Joseph:[1] try to find passages in the Gospels where Jesus might plausibly be reflecting Joseph. The exercise can only lead us closer to Jesus and to Joseph.

One obvious place to turn is prayers. In general, sons learn private prayers from their mothers—but within the household, in communal settings, from their fathers, who lead such prayers. Does the Lord's Prayer, then, reflect the common prayers in the household of the Holy Family, which Joseph led?

It also helps to have some kind of "instrument" or "method" of investigation. Here's one. Suppose we take the Patriarch Joseph to be a "type" of Saint Joseph, as the Church has traditionally believed and as popes have taught. For example, Leo XIII in *Quamquam Pluries* (Encyclical on Devotion to St. Joseph, August 15, 1889) says this:

> The Joseph of ancient times, son of the patriarch Jacob, was the type of St. Joseph.... The first Joseph won the favor and especial goodwill of his master.... Through Joseph's administration his household came to prosperity and wealth.... (Still more important) he presided over the kingdom with great power, and, in a time when the harvests failed, he provided for all the needs of the Egyptians with so much wisdom that the King decreed to him the title "Savior of the world." Thus it is that We may prefigure the new in the old patriarch.

[1] Published March 16, 2021.

Let us suppose that, even though Saint Joseph in Nazareth did not preside over great wealth and prosperity, nonetheless there was a magnanimity and magnificence in his character, which Our Lord as a child had noted and had wanted, then, to honor when He was a man, through imitation.

The obvious example would be the Marriage Feast of Cana. Saint John says explicitly that Mary was invited and that Jesus and the disciples accompanied her (Jn 2:1–2). This way of putting it seems meant to suggest that Joseph was no longer alive: Jesus accompanied His mother in Joseph's stead. What He did, then, may naturally be taken to be "in Joseph's stead", in imitation.

His care for the newly married couple, shown in His creation of about eight hundred bottles of the finest wine, seems exactly a realization of what the patriarch did, while also being a type of what Saint Joseph still does today for the Church, as Universal Patron.

Take this to be the first obvious reflection of Saint Joseph in the actions of Our Lord. But would a second not be what Our Lord said from the Cross, when He turned to Saint John and conferred Mary to him, with "Behold, your mother", and Mary to Saint John, with "Behold, your son" (Jn 19:26–27).

Again, let us assume that Joseph was no longer alive. The Fathers say that that was one motive for Our Lord's taking care of His Mother in this way. But then cannot we also say that Jesus was also reflecting a prior conferral? When Joseph was dying, he would have entrusted Jesus to Mary, and Mary to Jesus, not to effect a bond, but to affirm it, as if "take care of each other." That Jesus had this act in mind and wanted to imitate His earthly father at the hour of His death seems eminently plausible.

When I was doing a radio interview last week about my recent book, which is an investigation of the "reflections" of Mary in the Gospel of John, my host asked whether Mary, in turn, reflects anything about Joseph, a fitting question for the Year of Saint Joseph. I fumbled and said something like, "As Mary is likened to the moon because she reflects God's light, maybe Joseph can be likened to the earth, which reflects the moonlight. After all, like the earth, Joseph is solid, grounded, and, in his humility, a foundation." I did not answer the question.

On second thought, now I might say, simply, married couples grow to be alike: to know Mary, then, must be to know Joseph.

But also, if we want to know Joseph better, then look to those places where, we can guess, the Son in Mary's presence is specifically aiming to be like him.

# 30

# Saint Joseph's Not Untimely Death

Saint Joseph was certainly not alive when Jesus began His public ministry. This, the tradition has always maintained, for four reasons.

First, after the public ministry begins, Joseph is never mentioned in the Gospels in connection with Jesus or Mary, nor with the broader family of the "brothers" or more properly "cousins" of the Lord. There is even some suggestion in the way people refer to Joseph that he is no longer alive: "Is not this the carpenter's son?" (Mt 13:55)

Second, why would Jesus have conferred Mary to John, to take her into his house (Jn 19:27), if Joseph were still alive?

Third, Simeon's prophecy of suffering—"a sword will pierce through your own soul also" (Lk 2:35)—pertains only to Mary, not Joseph.

Fourth, it was most fitting that Joseph should leave the scene before the Lord's public ministry, so that when Jesus taught about "my Father", it would always be clear of whom he was speaking.

I find this list of reasons itself fascinating. I was a Protestant once, and, as a Protestant, I was convinced that the Gospel could have a much-needed sharpness in confronting "the world" only if Christians based their beliefs solely on Scripture, not on "mere human tradition".

And yet what is the status of this truth, that "Joseph was not alive when Jesus began His public ministry"? It is not quite based on Scripture alone; and yet it is based on Scripture. Moreover, it is not a "mere human tradition". Surely, it is a pious tradition, at least, that is, it is something shared and handed down among those who look at the life of the Lord with the eyes of faith.

As a Protestant, too, I had no coherent notion of authority in the Church. Thus, I could draw no distinction between what Christians are bound to believe as "of the faith" (de fide) and what we are free to believe because it is well-grounded and widely held among pious and thoughtful Christians.

As a Catholic, now, I can say that this truth—that Joseph died prior to the public ministry—is not de fide. And then that understanding frees me up to affirm it with just that force: I can defend it as true, and profitable to believe, while not implying that others are bound to believe it, if they are not persuaded by my reasons.

Of that list of reasons, the fourth is the most fascinating to me. Did Joseph appreciate it himself? Did he understand that it was better for him to depart from the world before Jesus entered upon the public stage? Father Gasnier in his great book of meditations, *Joseph the Silent*, thinks so: "Because he was Joseph, he realized too that his presence might become an obstacle rather than a help to Jesus. The world must not believe any longer that he was Jesus' true father."[1]

If so, Joseph's death takes on an interesting meaning.

To see why, consider a second question: About how old was Joseph when he died? If he was old when he was married, he would have been very old when he died. There

---

[1] Michel Gasnier, *Joseph the Silent* (New York: P.J. Kennedy & Sons, 1962), p. 164.

are some ancient traditions, rooted in the apocryphal writings, that Joseph was an old man, previously married for over forty years, when he was espoused to Mary. Saint Epiphanius places him at ninety years old! But this view was vigorously rejected by Saint Jerome. And it is safe to say that fuller reflection in the Church over the centuries has sided with Saint Jerome.

The better opinion, I think, which I accept, is that he was a young man when he married Mary. It was the custom then that men would aim to be married in their late teens. His devotion to virginity, his own and Mary's, was rooted in the idealism of the young. No one would have supported the marriage of a ninety-year-old man to a teenage girl. And it is misguided to attribute his respect of Mary's virginity to senility, not virtue.

So let us suppose he was twenty when he married Mary: he would likely have been in his forties when he died. That is to say, Saint Joseph died an "early death", even for those days. He did not die from old age and its generalized weakness, but rather (we exclude violence) from some definite affliction that took him away.

Now put these two thoughts together: Joseph realized that it was best for him to depart the scene; and he died as a relatively young man, accepting his death, at just that time, as sent by God.

And now I think we come to some remarkable results. The first is that we can understand the death of Joseph to be in its own mysterious way a participation, through foreshadowing, of the Passion of the Lord—just like the death of John the Baptist and the martyrdom of the Holy Innocents.

The second is that he offered up his life without yet seeing what the life of Jesus was for. Thus, his death was marked by tremendous faith. He did not hear the Sermon on the Mount. He did not see Jesus turn water into wine, heal lepers, or raise Lazarus. He did not see the Passion or the Resurrection.

The third is that the new life in Christ that he was chosen to witness was, exactly, the life of working alongside Jesus as friend and living a domestic life with Mary. No wonder that, where Christian family life in its ordinariness has flourished, Saint Joseph has been fervently invoked!

Finally, we can understand why popes have appointed Saint Joseph for us as Patron of the Dying, because he is especially sensitive to our felt untimeliness of death: "O Lord, happily will I die at the moment, in the place, and in the way that you want."

"Let me die as did glorious Saint Joseph, accompanied by Jesus and Mary, pronouncing those sweetest of names, which I hope to extol for all eternity."

# Part IV

# Sex and Marriage

# 31

# The Gospels Begin with Sex

The four Gospels in the canonical arrangement begin with Matthew. And Matthew's Gospel begins with sex.

It is not a "genealogy". All those fumbling sermons notwithstanding by pastors trying to find something to say about, "A was the father of B, and B was the father of C, and C was the father of D" and so on and so forth. Those strange Semitic names are hard to pronounce, but, we are told, "they exhibit the fallen race we come from and our need to be redeemed." Or, "just look at the adulterers and prostitutes in his family!" Or, "how gracious that some women were included!"

All of these efforts, however well-intentioned, are based on poor translations and our own impoverished ideas about sex.

The truth, as I see it, is that the Gospels begin with sex. This should be enticing, not tedious, and even something one would want to be a little discreet about.

Let's begin with translations. The Greek does not say "Abraham was the father of Isaac." If I may be literal, it says "Abraham generated Isaac." Yes, as a result of his generating Isaac, he was the father of Isaac. Even: in generating Isaac, Abraham became the father of Isaac. But he still is the father of Isaac today, right? If we insisted on speaking of his fatherhood, which is the effect, why put the effect, which remains, in the past tense anyway?

Fatherhood is an office, a position, an enduring relationship. Generation is an act. Fatherhood is something one discovers. Generation is something one does. Fatherhood persists; generation takes place and then is completed.

Writers are told to avoid the passive voice because it is more remote than the active voice from the action. Every passive fact depends upon and is the result of something active, something that is taking place and is more vivid. They may be simultaneous, but the activity is prior, nonetheless. "This man is beloved of the gods" (as Plato pointed out in the *Euthyphro*) is true only because "the gods love this man." But the reverse is not the case. It is not the case that "the gods love this man" because "this man is beloved of the gods."

Abraham is (not "was") the father of Isaac because he generated Isaac; not, Abraham generated Isaac because he was the father of Isaac.

Now, I will tell you a secret: Abraham did not generate Isaac except by going into Sarah, one particular evening, at some definite time, and lying with Sarah. And if it had not been that evening, and that time, it would not have been Isaac whom he had generated. So to say "Abraham generated Isaac" is to say that Abraham embraced Sarah at just that time when Isaac and not someone else would have been generated.

To say that "Abraham generated Isaac, and Isaac generated Jacob," and so on, is to give a causal sequence, not a list of familial relationships. The difference between this fact, which Matthew relays, and the dead translation of the New American Bible (and others), is like the difference between a man who sets up a row of dominoes, knocks the first one down, and exclaims, "Now watch them all

fall!" (effectively, what Matthew writes), and someone
who long after the fact comes around and makes a list of
which domino was to the left of which (which is what the
NAB conveys).

The one thing we can be grateful for is that, mercifully,
we do not yet have "Abraham was the parent of Isaac."

Nor does "beget" really get at it. "Beget" does not (to
use the word literally) be-get the proper meaning. Beget
means to get or to acquire, with effort. It is one of those
strange English words beginning with the prefix "be-",
like "bemuse", "befriend", "belittle".

"Behave" belongs in this group also. It means to com-
port oneself, as if by habit—thus "have", intensified to
mean "to have so thoroughly as if by habitude". That is
why it is nonsense for psychologists to think they have removed reference to the soul by describing their discipline,
in pseudo-scientific language, as "the study of human behavior". It certainly is not the study of movement, of a
mass changing its location in space. That special kind of
thing that we call behavior ineluctably implies a soul.[1]

Yes, it is true that since its first occurrences in the thir-
teenth century, "begat" was customarily used for a father's
"getting for himself" with care and commitment a child,
and not the mother's role also in assisting this. In that sense,
it is a good match for the Greek word, which tends to
be used for the father's active role in generation, whereas
the mother is passive ("And Boaz generated Obed, from
Ruth", Mt 1:5; AT).

And yet "begat" does not convey the fullness of what the
Greek does. To generate is to cause to come into existence
a being with the full likeness or close to the full likeness

---

[1] I once said to one of my sons, "Behave!" He replied indignantly, "I *am*
hāve."

of the generator. To read Matthew's causal sequence with this meaning in mind is to "see" the likeness of Abraham being conveyed through those other "generations".

When you survey the causal sequence, bring in also the principle, commonly taken for granted, that the first member of a causal sequence exerts an influence throughout that sequence and even to a greater degree than subsequent members. When Matthew summarizes the sequence at verse 17, placing Abraham and David at the head of causal chains of generating, he is claiming that Jesus is in their likeness and, as man, "governed" by their acts of procreation.

"But the generation of Jesus was in the following manner" (Mt 1:18; AT). Now: not by a man, a human father who generates. No one came into Mary's chamber and "knew" her: "And he did not know her through the time up to which she bore a son" (Mt 1:25; AT).

The Gospels begin with sex. And also, significantly, with the absence of sex—He was the first of those born, "not of blood, nor of the will of the flesh, nor of the will of man, but of God" (Jn 1:14; DR).

# 32

# The Body Is for the Lord

I love to find details in the Gospel not often noticed and ponder whether they are in fact deeply significant. I share my thoughts with you, dear reader, to encourage you to read the Gospels habitually, to encounter the Lord there.

A detail that leapt out to me last week[1] was in the Gospel for the memorial of Saint Monica (August 27), when Jesus raises from the dead the only son of the widow from Naim (Lk 7:12–15). The detail is this: after raising the young man, as a distinct act, Jesus gives him to his mother. Here is the passage in the Douay-Rheims translation:

> And when he came nigh to the gate of the city, behold a dead man was carried out, the only son of his mother; and she was a widow: and a great multitude of the city was with her. Whom when the Lord had seen, being moved with mercy towards her, he said to her: Weep not. And he came near and touched the bier. And they that carried it, stood still. And he said: Young man, I say to thee, arise. And he that was dead, sat up, and began to speak. And he gave him to his mother [*dedit illum matri suae*].

On the feast of Saint Monica, we are to understand that this saint wept for her son as this widow did, and, through

[1] Published September 1, 2021.

her prayers, the Lord restored Saint Augustine to her by bringing him to life in the Catholic faith.

The Church proposes this interpretation to us on the authority of Saint Augustine. In book VI of *Confessions*, he describes how his mother had traveled across land and sea to be with him in Milan. Augustine had by then rejected the dualistic philosophy of Manicheanism, but he was not yet a Catholic. Thus, Monica was still sorrowful and yet confident: "She was weeping for me as dead, but going to be restored to life by you, and on the bier of her thought she was carrying me out, so that you might say to the son of the widow: 'Young man, I say to you arise' and he would revive and begin to speak, and you would hand him over [*traderes*] to his mother."[2]

Saint Augustine evidently agrees that the miracle is not complete until the Lord somehow confers the son upon the mother. It is not enough to raise him to life; he must additionally, now living, be given to his mother. And this makes great sense, if the mother's sorrow was the occasion of the Lord's mercy.

But here is my question: Does the Lord simply give the young man to the mother, or does he give him *back* to his mother?

You ask, what is the difference? It is this. If the Lord gives him *back* to the mother, He simply restores him to the state he was in before he died. The mother had continued to have some kind of claim on him. And the young man is raised so that the mother can get him back.

But if, in contrast, the Lord simply *gives* him to his mother, then it is implied that the young man, after he is raised, belongs to the Lord. All bets are off, so to speak, about whether the mother will then get him "back". The Lord

[2] Book 6, par. 1.

might just as well have asked the son to follow him, as a disciple, right then and there. The Lord's giving him to the mother becomes therefore, so to speak, an extra gift to the woman, added onto the gift of new life for the son.

Well, that is the detail I noticed. The Greek says, as the Vulgate and Douay-Rheims faithfully convey, that the Lord simply gave the son to the mother, not that he "gave him back". (By the way, the New American Bible and RSVCE preserve this construction faithfully. But strangely Knox in his translation added "gave him back".)

One wonders whether others raised from the dead by the Lord, or even beneficiaries of great miracles, for example, those who regained their sight, believed that as a result they belonged to Him—that He had "first dibs" on their lives going forward. The demoniac had to be told, for instance, to remain with his people and not follow the Lord, as he wanted and as perhaps he sensed intuitively he should (Mk 5:19).

My question seems like a small point at first, but it is not, because it bears upon how we understand our own lives as Christians and the relationship between family claims and the Christian vocation.

After all, Baptism is a death and resurrection. "This sacrament is called *Baptism*, after the central rite by which it is carried out: to baptize (Greek *baptizein*) means to 'plunge' or 'immerse'; the 'plunge' into the water symbolizes the catechumen's burial into Christ's death, from which he rises up by resurrection with him, as 'a new creature'" (*Catechism of the Catholic Church*, no. 1214). After Baptism, our lives and our bodies are not our own, but are the Lord's.

No doubt it can be presumed that an infant, after Baptism, is given to his parents by the Lord. And yet isn't this gift only temporary, and in the manner of a fiduciary? The parents do not really "get him back"—not in the way in which he was theirs by nature, although they receive him more fully in Christ.

And then I think of how John Paul II in *Familiaris Consortio* explained the vocation to marriage as a specification of Baptism. It is fundamentally the Lord, it would seem, who gives husband to wife and wife to husband: "Spouses are therefore the permanent reminder to the Church of what happened on the Cross; they are for one another and for the children witnesses to the salvation in which the sacrament makes them sharers".[3]

In marriage and in our very lives, like the widow of Naim, we are dealing with direct and personal gifts from the Lord. We are not our own. In such a realization the ideology of autonomy dies.

[3] Pope John Paul II, Apostolic Exhortation *Familiaris Consortio* (November 22, 1981), no. 13.

# 33

# Signs of Mutual Love

On the third finger of my left hand I wear a wedding ring, which I understand to be a sign of my love for and fidelity to my wife, Catherine.

Yet the words of the liturgy seem to say otherwise. After all, when I received this ring from my wife at our wedding, she said, "Take this ring as a sign of my love and fidelity." So I seem to be wrong in my understanding: the ring that I wear stands for *her* fidelity, not mine. Or does it? How should we resolve this problem?

One way out is just to change the words. I have seen it suggested on a popular wedding website, lacking official authorization, that the couple should use the words, "I, _____, take this ring as a sign of my love and fidelity"!

So there is unclarity, which people by their common sense try to correct. You might suspect the unclarity entered with the *Novus Ordo*. You would be right. The Extraordinary Form, much clearer, has a blessing, of the bride's ring only, by the priest:

> Bless, + O Lord, this ring, which we bless + in Thy name, that she who shall wear it, keeping true faith unto her spouse, may abide in Thy peace and in obedience to Thy will, and ever live in mutual love.

Notice the words do not mention the ring's being a "sign" of anything. There is only a purpose clause, "that she who shall wear it". The reason is that the ring is regarded as a "sacramental", that is, as something holy that has the conferred power to do what it signifies (like holy water). The ring, then, does not merely signify her fidelity: it is meant to assist her in being faithful. (We sense this: the man who takes off his wedding ring before entering a bar thereby forsakes heavenly help in remaining faithful.)

The blessing also mentions obedience to the will of God. A sensible person understands this. To be married is to accept a rule; it is to be constrained. One freely takes on a yoke—an "easy" and a "light" yoke, to be sure, which, if worn in the right spirit, brings with it much "peace". But it would be foolish to deny that a wedding ring is as much a pledge to a discipline of life as is a Roman collar.

There is a flaw, or shortcoming, even in the older ritual: the blessing refers to "mutual love", and yet only the husband gives a ring to the bride, not the reverse. (It was the common custom throughout Europe until the late 1800s for only the wife to wear a wedding ring.) The new rite, as we shall see, tries to remedy this.

In the Extraordinary Form, the priest gives the blessed ring to the groom, who gives it to the bride, using one of two formulas:

With this ring I thee wed, and I plight unto thee my troth.

or

With this ring I thee wed; this gold and silver I thee give; with my body I thee worship; and with all my worldly goods I thee endow.

Linguists call this sort of language a "performative", since the words both signify the action and serve to accomplish the action. What the words signify and effect is the perfection of the marriage covenant through the giving of a precious object, the ring.

The precious object need not even be a ring! A ring happens to be the precious object that in ancient cultures could easily and safely be kept with you always. But the "gold and silver" refers to coins that may additionally be given—to wit, the famous "arras" still given in the ceremony in Hispanic cultures and for that reason incorporated as an option in U.S. Catholic weddings in 2016.

Back in the day when marriage was more widely understood, not as a personal relationship simply, but as an institution that was a path to financial stability, the man's gift of a precious object to the woman was "earnest money" of his commitment to establishing this institution with her in particular. Moreover, one family or both would provide initial capital for the newly founded institution, the "dower". Since it remains true that marriage is that sort of institution, one might argue that the tradition of "arras", as a vestige and testimony to this understanding, would profitably be revived outside of Hispanic cultures, too.

We can now see, in contrast, the meaning of the words in the new rite. When the groom says, "Take this ring as a sign of my love and fidelity", he is referring not to the wearing of the ring, but to the gift of the ring as a precious object. He confers the ring out of love and with pledged fidelity; afterward, she wears the ring out of love and as a pledge of fidelity. (In 2016, the language was changed to: "Receive this ring ..."—not "Take this ring ..."—which arguably helps to remedy the problem by emphasizing better the one-time act of conferral.)

So is the new language confused, confusing—or (perhaps inadvertently) deeply true? Ask yourself this: Is a wedding ring in modern contexts the whole object or half an object? Compare: a shoe is half an object, not a whole object, since shoes come in pairs. Clearly, today we do conceive of wedding rings as similarly coming in pairs, so that, strictly, one person does not wear "a ring", but two wear a single object—"the rings"—with two locations in space. Thus, each ring, especially as it is incomplete on its own, signifies the love and fidelity of both.

Thus, the words of the new rite, despite their initial unclarity perhaps, turn out to be deeply true. A thing often signifies its provenance. That ring on my left hand never ceases to "say" that it was received as a sign of love and fidelity. And as worn, it signifies love and fidelity that are precisely reciprocated and mutual.

# 34

# Is Once Enough?

The marital act has both a unitive and a procreative meaning—this we are told authoritatively in *Humanae Vitae*, whose fiftieth anniversary is tomorrow,[1] but not only there. And we are also told that these meanings are inseparable. If so, it would follow that couples who think they are getting the unitive dimension on its own, by using contraception, are deceived and not getting it at all. They have changed what appear to be acts of love into a mere coordination of egoisms (as Karol Wojtyła argued famously in his book *Love and Responsibility*).

A single marital act, however, seems enough for the procreative meaning of the act to have its full force—namely, when a child is conceived. The couple comes together just once, and, as it happens, they have successfully procreated. So, if the unitive and procreative meanings are inseparable, does it follow that a single marital act can be enough, too, for its unitive meaning to have full force?

I want to argue that it does, not merely for its own sake, but to help refute a heresy of the day. According to that heresy, when couples get married, they should want two things: to beget and raise children, and to enjoy a lifetime of sexual satisfaction. Call this second thing "sexual companionship",

<hr>

[1] This essay was published on July 24, 2018.

"a good sex life", or "continual intimacy"—or whatever. The heresy is to say that this second thing, or the marital act's contribution to this, is what is meant by the unitive dimension.

Some people even say that a married couple has a right to "sexual satisfaction". But since pregnancy, childbirth, and the stresses of parenting are plainly at odds with this "sexual satisfaction", it looks like contraception is needed to balance the two, in what gets called "responsible parenthood".

For this heresy, once is not enough—no number of times is ever enough. The sex act has a purely progressive meaning, as contributing to an ongoing life of sexual fulfillment. The next act is always necessary to continue this satisfaction and, even, to prove it. The past act must appear to count for nothing.

But once is enough as regards the most important unity in marriage, whereby they become two in one flesh:

> A valid marriage between the baptized is called ratified only if it has not been consummated; it is called ratified and consummated if the spouses have performed between themselves in a human fashion a conjugal act which is suitable in itself for the procreation of offspring, to which marriage is ordered by its nature and by which the spouses become one flesh. (CIC 1061 §1)

And clearly there are many couples for whom once was enough for every kind of unity. You probably know couples—my uncle and aunt were like this—he was a soldier, and she his high school sweetheart. They got married just before he was deployed to Europe during World War II. He spent three years away.

Assume for argument's sake their honeymoon night was one night only. Would not the consummation of that one night—or their marriage as viewed through that lens— have been enough for him to claim, for all those years, every form of marital union? So that he would have a strong reason to refuse to visit prostitutes or to flirt with the girls in French towns?

The case is even stronger, of course, if a child is conceived. In the movie *The Natural*, Iris (the Glenn Close character) sends Roy Hobbs (Robert Redford) a note, saying to the messenger, "I have his son in the stands. He does not know his son is here." When Hobbs (in the on-deck circle) reads the note and realizes that his one embrace of this woman fourteen years before had conceived a child, he does not weigh having a son with her against lack of sexual satisfaction with her through their years of separation—as if the lack in the one respect could touch the unity in the other respect. We would despise him if he did. Rather, in the movie, he must deliberately reject as a false, competing ideal the sexual companionship promised by Memo (Kim Basinger).

The "once is enough" attitude is retrospective as well as prospective. A pure-hearted man, during courtship, longs to be joined with his beloved. When he gains her, he takes custody of that union in his heart. What before was longing becomes gratitude afterward. Gratitude is never static. But each subsequent union on this understanding is free rather than compelled. There is no need to constitute anything—continual sexual satisfaction—because the one-flesh unity of the marriage already exists, which the couple will naturally want to memorialize and restate.

I said that it "seems" that the procreative meaning can attain its full force in a single marital act. Actually not: because procreation for human beings is not the mere conception of a new life but also the raising and educating of that being over something like twenty years. Thus, the procreative meaning is not something inert; it must be elicited by the deliberate will of the parents, cooperating together. But in the same sense it can fulfill the unitive sense, if the parents deliberately choose to see that growing child as the embodiment of their one-flesh union.

We cannot discuss the good direction of the will and "seeing" things in the right way without bringing in the virtues. That is why it is a calumny to say, as some do, against the magisterial teaching of John Paul II, that he failed to appreciate the difficulties of married couples needing to abstain.

What I have called the heresy of sexual satisfaction, he refers to as "concupiscence". He concludes his famous catechesis on theology of the body with a lengthy discussion of the virtue of "continence" in the service of "conjugal chastity", which "gradually reveals itself as a singular capacity to perceive, love, and practice those meanings of the language of the body which remain altogether unknown to concupiscence itself".[2]

---

[2] John Paul II, General Audience (October 24, 1984), translated in *L'Osservatore Romano (English Edition)*, October 29, 1984, p. 1.

## 35

# Food Not Sex

I have heard Catholics, usually men, wonder whether the reception of Holy Eucharist can be compared to the marital embrace. (Women in contrast seem to find it natural to liken it to pregnancy, to bearing the Christ child within, like Mary.)

This seemingly male intimation has found perhaps its most explicit formulation in some accounts of the "Theology of the Body". For example, one popularizer has written:

> Catholicism sees the whole relationship between God and Man in quasi-sexual terms. John Paul II describes the Eucharist as "the sacrament of the Bridegroom and the Bride" (*Mulieris Dignitatem*, no. 26). This "one flesh" communion of a husband and wife (Christ and the Church) lies at the heart of our belief and worship. It's the source and summit of our faith.... Oh glorious exchange! Oh wondrous nuptials! Through the Incarnation, Christ has wed Himself to our humanity so that we might be wed to His divinity. And we consummate this marriage, where else? In the Eucharist.[1]

---

[1] Christopher West, "The Scandal of the Body". Republished on the website of Fred Fredosso at the University of Notre Dame: https://www3.nd.edu/~afredos/papers/cwest-tob.htm, accessed February 4, 2025.

The Eucharist, then, is characterized as the act of consummation of the marriage of divinity to humanity in the Incarnation.

The flip side of the comparison, of course, is that something so problematized as sexual relations in marriage gets analogized to something so unproblematic, in the spiritual life, as Holy Communion. And if the popes have recommended daily reception of the Eucharist, well ... it is an inference that many husbands, to be sure, would like to draw.

Now *sed contra* to these analogies would seem to be the instincts of the saints. In the hymns of Saint Thomas Aquinas, the Eucharist is compared with the pelican mother's blood, living bread, the hidden divinity of Christ on the Cross, God to be seen face-to-face, and the infant Christ. But not a hint of the marital embrace. Christ's face only is revealed, and that by the lifting of a veil upon our death. A steadfast friend will greet us then, not a lover.

Again, hardly any prayer can be imagined to be more erotic (*sensu stricto*) than Saint Bonaventure's prayer after Communion: "Pierce the very marrow of my soul with the delightful, health-giving dart of Thy love.... May it ever desire to be dissolved and to be with Thee."[2] Yet the saint instructs us to pray that our souls may ever hunger for the Bread of Angels and thirst for the Fount of wisdom and knowledge—not yearn for a quasi-marital joining.

Upon reflection, it makes sense that, whatever one's subjective imaginations, the Eucharist is called food and not profitably compared with sex.

First of all, there is no such thing as a "yearning for sex". In reality, by nature, and originally, there is the desire of union with a man for a woman, and with a woman for a

---

[2] Origin unknown of this common translation of St. Bonaventure's famous prayer.

man. As the sexes are complementary, so there are two complementary urges. Hence, it is an illusion to imagine that there could be a common and shared desire for the Eucharist, along these lines, among male and female Christians. And yet men and women hunger and thirst in the same way.

Again, the marital embrace is of its nature exclusive, but the Eucharist embraces and unites all who partake of it. Saint John Chrysostom wrote, "To him we unite ourselves, and we are made one body, one flesh."[3] Tellingly, the saint emphasizes not that we are made one flesh with the Lord, but rather that we are made one flesh with one another (although to be sure the one is the reason for the other). One might wonder whether the comparison with the marital embrace does not attract us precisely because, in contrast, it is inherently individualistic: it is *I myself* who finds consummation in the Eucharist.

Again, the consummation of marriage in the marital embrace occurs only once. If one had to say what suited the nature of the marital embrace more, "once" or "daily", surely it would be once. Once consummates a marriage; once can beget a child. Sin gives witness also: one illicit embrace proves disloyalty and constitutes adultery, while one chaste embrace is a sufficient pledge of fidelity. A woman's body has its own receptivity that changes over a month. And yet: "Give us this day our daily bread." Each of us needs three meals each day.

Again, children surely are as capable of grasping the mystery of the Eucharist as much as adults—insofar as any of us can at all. But food makes sense to them—how could sex possibly do so? The Virgin Mary and any virgin would

---

[3] Quoted in Alphonsus Maria de Liguori, *The Passion and the Death of Jesus Christ*, ed. Eugene Grimm (Brooklyn: Redemptorist Fathers, 1927), p. 55.

presumably have nothing to do with the imagery of sexual embrace. Too many of us ought to be innocent when we are not, and, for those, the sexual embrace can be bound up with compunction, regret, and shame.

Then consider the incidents of consuming food. Food is "completely given" as corporeal because it is consumed and "lost" in the reception and in the gift. But despite the language of "total gift of self", no one's body is given in this way in the marital embrace.

Indeed, one might argue that, if the image of food already captures the fact that He poured Himself out for us completely, then there's nothing lacking in the image, nothing further to be represented by matter to our senses. "O divine food, Sacrament of love, when wilt Thou draw me entirely to Thyself?" Saint Alphonsus Liguori asks. "Thou has nothing left to do in order to make Thyself loved by me."[4] In the order of final causes, it is the very purpose of food, not sex, to reveal the sacrament.

The comparison with sex, then, does not add but detracts. "In order that he might not be separated from us even by death," Liguori explains, "he would leave us his whole self as food ... giving us to understand by this that, having given us this gift of infinite worth, he could give us nothing further to prove to us his love."[5]

"When we think of this love," Saint Mary Magdalen of Pazzi would tell her novices, "we cannot pass on to other thoughts, but must stop upon love."[6]

[4] Ibid., p. 55.
[5] Ibid., p. 52.
[6] As reported by St. Alphonsus, ibid., p. 53.

# 36

# The Marriage Problem
# and Its Solution

The marriage problem among Catholics, historically, was that the wife, out of fear of childbearing, showed "the coldness of Chloe", while the man for good and bad reasons strongly desired his wife: a standoff leading to anger, frustration, and recrimination.

Childbearing was indeed something to be afraid of. Parish records in England show that around 1850, for example, the mother died in one out of twenty births. If the husband was risking his life at war or in a dangerous job for the sake of his family, there was parity. But otherwise one might at least raise a doubt about the quality of love that asks for a potential sacrifice of the life of the other but not oneself.

The language "Husbands, love your wives, as Christ loved the Church, and gave himself up for her," therefore, raised a serious challenge (Eph 5:25). How exactly was he to do that?

There are lots of reasons for Chloe to be cold, or at least cool, even when maternal mortality has dropped, as now, to one-fiftieth of the risk it used to have, such as fatigue and worry, persistent exhaustion, the need for recovery or a break, a different biology and different imperatives—and perhaps even a more proportioned view of sex.

After all, the relationship of intimacy to offspring, the greater good surely, will be clearer to the wife. And there are many more causes from the culture for the husband to feel himself frustrated and aggrieved, obviously. In natural and sacramental marriage, then, the marriage problem remains.

Probably "theology of the body"—in its popular forms—aggravates the problem by creating unrealistic expectations. Marriage is not a repeated reenactment of the ecstasy of the internal life of the Trinity. Natural Family Planning does not itself solve anything, but draws greater attention to the problem, because it rules out relations just at the time when the wife is most likely to be drawn to them—which can even seem perverse, hardly "natural".

Putting the best face on it, we might redescribe the marriage problem as the tension between romance and marriage. Romance outside of marriage has a way of turning itself into sex. One sad solution but so common as almost to characterize entire cultures (umm, France) was the mistress.

In less hypocritical but more deceitful, yet "sincere", societies, such as ours, the husband might favor a series of affairs. Or pornography will appear to be the way out—promiscuity and porn in many cases simply being the easy path, the husband returning to old habits from college.

In simpler times, say, around 1950, after Catholics got married, they regarded themselves as fixed in that marriage for life, not for any particular reason except that the Catholic Church in her wisdom, apart from all the other Christian "denominations", insisted on it. These Catholics of course experienced all of the tensions of what I am calling the marriage problem. But it was a problem you were stuck with. You did not complain, and you gritted it out somehow.

Now present them with The Pill. Unlike other methods, it works invisibly. One does not seem to be deliberately doing anything to block conception in using it. It requires no choice in the moment. It comes with the calm assurance of Science, the same people who gave us the polio vaccine.

Then consider this fact about anger: it is easily transferred. What could be more arbitrary, unreasonable, and cruel, than that a Church—that "expert in humanity"!—which forbids divorce and locks us into this relationship (understand that each couple facing the marriage problem thinks that they are the only ones), now, for incomprehensible reasons, tells us that we cannot use this Scientifically Recommended, "obviously" suitable solution to our problems?

What exactly does a priest say to a couple who week after week complains to him angrily in this way? They are married, after all, and he has no experience. What did the "Birth Control Commission" appointed by Saint Pope Paul VI do, when couples from the United States lobbied by compiling story after story of couples whose marriage, they said, was on the rocks because of the inevitable frustrations of following the Church's teaching?

They mainly caved, of course. Faced with anger, if one is kind, one caves. Yet the saint who was pope did not, nor did the saint who was on the minority side of the commission.

Of course, everything unravels once artificial birth control is accepted. Marriage changes its meaning. Courtship disappears. Abortion, already implicit in contraception and explicit in some methods, follows immediately. People in same-sex relationships understandably look on and ask why what is good for these others is not also good for them.

Looking back at the consequences, it can seem now as if the couples who were angrily lobbying the Vatican wanted all of society to be overturned to solve their problem—that a private good would take precedence over the common good.

And in that crisis and strain the archbishop of Krakow crafted his lectures on *Love and Responsibility*. His goal, he said, was to show how love as *eros* finds a place in love as *caritas*—to solve the marriage problem, the tension between romance and marriage. If the family is the basic cell of society and marriage the foundation of the family, then it is not too much to say that this teaching is the main contribution of his pontificate for the Church—and for mankind.

Like all other genuine problems, the marriage problem has no natural solution. We can avoid it—we can "destroy the mystery", as other ages tried to avoid the Incarnation or Trinity by asserting only half of the truth. That is the spectacle we see today, among many if not perhaps most of the members of the hierarchy, just as outrageous as other acts of denial in the history of the Church.

Or we can accept that marriage offers no genuine joy except what comes through the Cross and rediscover and embrace that Cross daily.

# 37

# Lambeth Ninety Years Later[1]

The Lambeth Conference of 1930 subverted itself, everyone agrees, but how? That is the question.

Some background: the Church of England, spread throughout the world by the British Empire, felt the need, beginning in the 1850s, to hold worldwide conferences of bishops for the sake of unity. These meetings were convened about every ten years at the London residence of the archbishop of Canterbury, Lambeth Palace.

The Lambeth Conference of 1930 was infamous, even in its day, for its Resolution 15 on artificial contraception:

Where there is a clearly felt moral obligation to limit or avoid parenthood the method must be decided on Christian principles. The primary and obvious method is complete abstinence from intercourse (as far as may be necessary) in a life of discipline and self-control lived in the power of the Holy Spirit. Nevertheless in those cases where there is such a clearly felt moral obligation to limit or avoid parenthood, and where there is a morally sound reason for avoiding complete abstinence, the Conference agrees that other methods may be used, provided that this is done in the light of the same Christian principles. The Conference records its strong condemnation of the use of

[1] Published September 1, 2020.

any methods of conception-control from motives of self-ishness, luxury, or mere convenience.[2]

The resolution, which passed 193 to 67 with 47 abstentions, is said to be the first instance where any responsible authority—not simply in Christendom but in any culture—had publicly supported, in any way at all, the use of artificial contraception. Pope Pius XI was so distressed by this defection from, we may say, the common view of humanity in the natural law, that he wrote his encyclical *Casti Connubii* in reply.

The resolution was infamous even in its day because it flatly contradicted the Lambeth Conference of 1920:

> We utter an emphatic warning against the use of unnatural means for the avoidance of conception, together with the grave dangers—physical, moral and religious—thereby incurred ... we steadfastly uphold what must always be regarded as the governing considerations of Christian marriage. One is the primary purpose for which marriage exists, namely the continuation of the race through the gift and heritage of children; the other is the paramount importance in married life of deliberate and thoughtful self-control.[3]

Indeed, how could unity across space possibly be fostered by a body that did not maintain unity over time?

The main holding of Resolution 15 in a very short time subverted the "strong condemnation" at the end of the

---

[2] "Lambeth Conference 1930: Resolution 15", Anglican Communion, accessed June 3, 2025, https://www.anglicancommunion.org/resources/document-library/lambeth-conference/1930/resolution-15-the-life-and-witness-of-the-christian-community-marriage.

[3] "Lambeth Conference 1920: Resolution 68", Anglican Communion, accessed June 3, 2025, https://www.anglicancommunion.org/resources/document-library/lambeth-conference/1920/resolution-68-problems-of-marriage-and-sexual-morality.aspx.

paragraph. But the other "strong" teachings of the conference were likewise subverted:

—Resolution 16: The Conference further records its abhorrence of the sinful practice of abortion.
—Resolution 17: [The Conference] ... condemns the propaganda which treats contraception-control as a way of meeting those unsatisfactory social and economic conditions which ought to be changed by the influence of Christian public opinion.
—Resolution 18: Sexual intercourse between persons who are not legally married is a grievous sin.[4]

That resolution went on to say that, to thwart the "increasing use of contraceptives among the unmarried and the extension of irregular unions owing to the diminution of any fear of consequences, the Conference presses for legislation forbidding the exposure for sale and unrestricted advertisement of contraceptives."[5]

Now, note that this was the "bad" Lambeth Conference. And yet one can hardly find even a Catholic bishop today who will make similar strong condemnations and take such a position about received law—against our *Griswold* and our *Eisenstadt*. Neither do the new advocates of the "common good" dare to express this view: it is much bolder to tax and regulate economic activity, right?

T. S. Eliot gave his theory of how the conference would subvert itself in an essay, "Thoughts after Lambeth". Resolution 15 was "almost suicidal", he opined. But why? Not because it subjects practical reasoning to the internal unraveling that must follow upon holding that something intrinsically wrong was permissible. Indeed, Eliot shows

---

[4] See the Resolutions Archives of the 1930 Lambeth Conference at https://www.anglicancommunion.org/media/127734/1930.pdf.
[5] Ibid., no. 11.

himself confused about the distinction between proximate end (the means of avoiding conception) and remote end (the grounds for wanting to avoid conception). That is, he never grasps the teaching of the Roman Church, which he opposes.

Rather, he argued that the bishops had intended to permit the use of artificial contraception for only a small number of cases—where the couple feels a genuine perplexity of conscience. And yet the bishops give no grounds for identifying cases like that: "To allow that 'each couple' should take counsel only if perplexed in mind is almost to surrender the whole citadel of the Church. It is ten to one, considering the extreme disingenuity of humanity, which ought to be patent to all after so many thousand years, that only a very small minority will be 'perplexed'," Eliot wrote, "and then ten-to-one as well that, if they seek advice from a clergyman, they'll be told anything other than 'do what you like.' "[6]

The *Washington Post* had its own diagnosis. It editorialized, not on the Lambeth Conference precisely, but on a committee of the Federal Council of Churches in America, which copied Lambeth and passed a similar resolution in 1931.

In sentences that seem as if lifted from *Humanae Vitae* and transported back in time, the WaPo editors wrote that "the committee's report if carried into effect would sound the death-knell of marriage as a holy institution, by establishing degrading practices which would encourage indiscriminate immorality." Repeating Eliot's argument, they added: "The suggestion that the use of legalized contraceptives would be 'careful and restrained' is preposterous" (March 22, 1931).

---

[6] T. S. Eliot, *Thoughts after Lambeth* (London: Faber & Faber, 1931), p. 17.

One reads this and is shocked to realize that it spontaneously identifies artificial contraception with the shady culture of prostitutes and the like.

The problem is bad education, the WaPo editors suggest: these churchmen "struggle ... with adhering to Christian doctrine while at the same time indulging in amateurish excursions into the fields of economics, legislation, medicine, and sociology", peddling "a mixture of religious obscurantism and modernistic materialism".

Ninety years later, it looks as though only John Paul II's papacy did anything to slow the slide, the corporate suicide of a civilization.

# 38

# Contraception and Our Abdication
of Fatherhood

In the Year of Saint Joseph,[1] the celebration of Father's
Day last Sunday stands, to the days that come after it, in
much the same way as a feast day like Easter Sunday conditions the "ordinary time" in the rest of the year. This
year, fatherhood is simply too important a topic of reflection to relegate to one Sunday in early summer. On such
a premise, I want to investigate the connection between
contraception and fatherhood.

My thesis is that contraception negates fatherhood, is
at war with it, undermines what it means to be a father.
Where widely adopted, it works out that effect in all aspects
of society. We are familiar with the idea, championed by
Saint John Paul II, "the Great", that contraception attacks
the unity of husband and wife. The unitive dimension
of the sexual act will not survive, he taught, if separated
from the procreative. I want to add: fatherhood will not
survive if the sexual act is separated from its fatherly aspect.

That contraception negates fatherhood should be obvious on its face. A man places himself in a position where
he can declare for or against becoming a father: he declares

---

[1] Published June 24, 2021.

CONTRACEPTION AND OUR ABDICATION OF FATHERHOOD 175

against. He deliberately removes the possibility of fatherhood from the act designed to make him a father.

(Note that by this language of "declaring against", it is easy to distinguish Natural Family Planning from contraception. Someone who practices Natural Family Planning, while perhaps refraining from "declaring for", depending on his ultimate purpose, never "declares against". Natural Family Planning is like silence on the issue, and silence is interpreted as consent.)

Suppose we say that fatherhood represents the perfection, the full realization, of what it means to be a male. This is plausible because the sexual power is the sole complementary power, of its essence, of men and woman. To be a man is to be such as to procreate with a woman; to be a woman is to be such as to procreate with a man.

We can use more shocking language, but language that our forebears had no difficulty with (read Matthew 1): to be a man is to be such as to beget in a woman; to be a woman is to be such as to bear what is begotten by a man. This is why the language of *Theotokos*, or "bearer of what is begotten by God", is so much more suggestive than "Mother of God"—because it clearly expresses the complementarity of human and divine nature, which was effected precisely through the Incarnation.

If these things are so, then, when a man declares against fatherhood, he declares against his masculinity, too. By deliberately removing the core of fatherhood from his action, which is the core of his masculinity, he effectively agrees to the redefinition of his masculinity by something connected with, but incidental, to it.

We live in a society where women think they become men by taking on characteristics incidental to masculinity. But for decades men, negating their fatherhood in contraception, have been re-identifying and repackaging themselves as men in the same way—by how they dress, by how they act, by the shape of their bodies. If you are a man and you practice contraception, then, arguably, the label "cisgender male" does not entirely miss the mark for you; at least, there's something deeply correct about it.

He declares not only against his masculinity, however, but also against his relationship with God, by cutting God off from the matter—because God is the source of his authority as a man. And in cutting off God, he undermines his own authority as a man. Let me explain this important thought.

We cannot know the future; it is unreasonable to make representations about the future except in matters that depend directly on our control: hence our commitments reaching far into the future should be few, and the fact that they are unconditional ("for better or for worse, in sickness and in health"), surprisingly, makes them better able to be kept, because then they are insulated from contingency.

But to consent to the conception of a new being, through one's own actions, is to make oneself responsible for an undertaking of nurturing and educating that child that reaches at least twenty years into the future. Since we cannot know the future, such an undertaking is reasonable only if it is regarded as a joint undertaking with someone who does know that future, that is, if we regard it as done with the approval and blessing of God in His Providence.

That is to say, for a father to conceive a child in openness to life is for him to place himself under God: he recognizes himself as a subsidiary source of life and, therefore, since he has become a subsidiary agent, he enjoys a subsidiary authority.

But look what happens if he uses contraception and conceives a child only—he thinks—when he has sufficient control over his circumstances. Rejecting reliance upon God, he has replaced authority with the very different realities of control and power. His authority, if he had claimed it, would have been inherent in his "office" as father. But his control and power, notoriously, are shifting and cannot be counted on. Moreover, the field of power is vast, and a local power is easily swamped by large-scale external forces or overtaken by a more general power—the government, for example.

No genuine authority is ever lost through being taken away; all genuine authority is abdicated before it is taken away. We can look throughout our society and see many signs that might lead a perceptive observer to conclude that genuine fatherhood no longer exists. I will not detail them here but leave that exercise to your discrete consideration.

One might blame the Supreme Court, the media, the market, or a "culture of expressive individualism" for this. These have indeed worked to take away the authority of fathers. But what if men had abdicated that authority first?

# 39

# Babes and Alms

"I was hungry and you gave me food, I was thirsty and you gave me drink, I was a stranger and you welcomed me" (Mt 25:35).

"As you did it to one of the least of these my brethren, you did it to me" (Mt 25:40).

The most natural objects today of these familiar verses from Matthew 25 are children. A baby cries from hunger and thirst: the mom nurses the baby. The toddler grows out of his shoes in a couple of months: the parents sacrifice to replace them.

And the baby in the womb in our society counts as a "stranger". A philosopher, Judith Jarvis Thomson, wrote a famous article on this premise. A woman discovering that she is pregnant, Thomson argued, is like someone waking up to find that a stranger has been hooked up to her for life support. You would not have an obligation to keep that stranger alive, she claims, and neither does a mom have any obligations to her unborn child.

As twisted and misguided as this view is, it is the implicit premise, nonetheless, of legal abortion. The precious son or daughter by societal convention turned into a complete stranger to be disposed of at will. Who counts better as "these least of my brethren"?

But since these verses from Matthew 25 have traditionally also defined the main corporal works of mercy, the question arises of whether, today, we need a new understanding of almsgiving so that what Christian parents typically do counts as giving alms in the strict sense.

The case is even stronger for the spiritual works of mercy. Who instructs the ignorant more than a mom? Who reproves the sinner more than a dad? Who "bears with those who trouble and annoy us" more than a mom and dad, not only with each other, but also with the child who vomits in the back of the car, has a tantrum in church, will not eat his dinner, or keeps dropping his socks on the stairway?

I say "Christian" parent because almsgiving, by definition, is an act relieving the need of another carried out, deliberately, in fulfillment of the two great precepts of charity: to love God with one's whole being, and to love one's neighbor as oneself. For a Christian, love of the child, baptized and therefore identified with Christ, is at once love of God and love of another self.

A typical older definition shows an unfortunate tendency to construe almsgiving as a relationship between classes. "Any material favor that assists the needy, prompted by charity, is almsgiving." So begins the entry in the old Catholic Encyclopedia. Its treatment is excellent, of course, and yet as this language of "the needy" shows, it tends to think of objects of almsgiving as belonging to classes of needy persons ("refugees", "victims of the hurricane", "the blind") who are aided by dedicated, organized efforts of other classes ("the wealthy", "the churches"). Such groups exist, of course, and sometimes not merely by abstraction (whole nations may be in great need, such as Ukraine right now). And yet, the central case of almsgiving is of one person helping another, each the "neighbor" or "brother" of the other: look again at Matthew 25.

We can perhaps get at this needed, broader understanding of almsgiving by contrast. There are other ways of addressing needs in our society, after all: I have in mind market exchanges. When the butcher goes to the baker for bread, he brings meat with him (or money as a proxy) to address the need of the baker, who gives bread in exchange, which addresses the need of the butcher. A market exchange is one where each addresses the need of the other with a view to receiving something equally back.

Therefore, construe almsgiving as any addressing of another's need (out of love of God and neighbor), which is not so compensated. "For if you love those who love you, what reward have you?" (Mt 5:46). That is, in a market exchange each gets precisely and only what he trades for. "But when you give a feast, invite the poor, the maimed, the lame, the blind, and you will be blessed, because they cannot repay you" (Lk 14:13–14). That is, deliberately enter into "exchanges" that are not like that, because the counterparty is incapable of compensating you. But every family dinner is like this: it is a "feast" where the poor are invited, who "have not wherewith" to pay for the meal as at a restaurant.

"The world" does not see family relationships in this way, because "the world", deeply misguided, looks upon children as commodities or as means for fulfilling the aspirations of the parents. Thus, the parents feeding their children at dinner, in the example just given, on that misguided understanding are just consoling themselves. "They have their reward" right then and there. But Christians reject this understanding. They see children as gifts of God, belonging to God, temporarily in their care—who are just as incapable of fulfilling the happiness of their parents as any fallen, finite creature.

To be sure, governmental tax and education policies need to be radically revised to assist parents raising children. But before that let's also get the Christian incentives right, by acknowledging parents as exemplary givers to babes of alms.

# 40

# Welcoming the Stranger

"I was a stranger and you welcomed me" (Mt 25:35).

Who are strangers, and who are family? If every member of the human race is my brother and sister, then strangers are family. If so, are family also strangers?

It seems so. Take children. What can be more "family" than children? Therefore, if children are strangers, all family are strangers.

Begin with a married couple who adopt a child. They are surely welcoming a stranger. The child they adopt is not theirs by blood. He or she was carried and probably nurtured at the very start by someone else. He or she was unfamiliar to them and then was welcomed in.

We admire adoptive parents. More than this, we intuit that they tell us something about all parents, about the very essence of parenting. And this would seem to be one truth they testify to: that even our children "by blood" do not belong to us. We are merely fiduciaries and will need to give an account of our trust to the Most High.

So much holds for all children everywhere. But it holds especially of Christians, who most of all are begotten "not of blood nor of the will of the flesh nor of the will of man, but of God" (Jn 1:13). They are begotten of God in Baptism, which confers supernatural life. If infinity is to finitude as any whole number to zero, then relation by blood fades to insignificance when compared with the eternity opened up, like the heavens, in any child's Baptism. C.S. Lewis said, "You have never talked to a mere mortal."[1] Yet it was a mere mortal animal that begot this child.

Now, this child being brought to Baptism is a pagan. Yes, that child swaddled in white at the Church where everyone is dressed up and gathered around is unlike everyone else there in being a pagan, pure and simple. I take it that pagans are in some important sense strangers to Christians, as such.

So to welcome any child at all, not simply by adoption, is to welcome a stranger, and this becomes infinitely true when the child is welcomed in Baptism.

I take it that "welcoming" does not mean just the first opening of the door. Jesus, a stranger, knocks; you let Him in. A couple of hours later, you throw Him out or argue with Him so violently that He wishes to leave. "But I welcomed you, Lord." This would now be false. Welcoming implies a lasting state.

There is no need to draw exact analogies here with, say, headstrong or moody teenagers—always difficult cases. That is not my point. My point is simply that, "until death do us part", the mother or father continues to welcome the stranger precisely in caring for their child. The child, although family, remains someone who "once a stranger, was welcomed".

This one realization helps us to understand why charity really does begin at home, in the sense that the love that should typically be shown in a household is in no sense secondary to the putative extraordinary altruism of care

---

[1] C.S. Lewis, *The Weight of Glory and Other Addresses* (New York: Macmillan, 1949), p. 15.

for "strangers". Rather, it is primary. And you and I know
it has its difficulties and challenges. All social concern is
shown first in welcoming the child.

But now let's think of husband and wife. "Bone of my
bone and flesh of my flesh"? "They shall be two in one
flesh"? "He who loves his wife loves himself"? Who could
be less of a stranger, the one to the other? Actually, in
Christian marriage, strictly, there is not even "the one"
and "the other".

I take it that Adam's rib was alienated from him once it
was removed from his body. Of course, the woman had
to become "other" first for her to be a companion at all.

The Bible didactically refers to women who are potentially one's wife, but not so as "strange women". But
when it comes to other cases, "King Solomon loved many
strange women" (1 Kings 11:1; DR). "A strange woman is
a narrow pit" (Prov 23:27; DR). "And why wilt thou, my
son, be ravished with a strange woman, and embrace the
bosom of a stranger?" (Prov 5:20; KJV). The same Hebrew
word means alien, foreign, other.

This shows that marriage (and only marriage!) makes it
so that a man and woman are not "strange" in that sense
to each other. (And in this fact is contained everything one
needs to say about "knowing another" outside of marriage.)
But then by the same token, before marriage—no matter
how long they courted or were engaged—the wife was a
"stranger" to the husband and the husband to the wife.

When they got married, then, each welcomed a stranger.
If they are separated or divorced (let me put it this way,
to avoid the appearance of imputing blame in complicated
and delicate matters): materially there has been some failure
in "welcoming the stranger". Contrariwise, and positively,
a couple who stay together despite difficulties testify together to the Christian ideal of "welcoming the stranger".

We are looking for charity in all the wrong places.

One more application: to Christians we take for granted. I do not take them for granted, but I fear many clerics do. You know, the Christians who come to daily Mass, hand out holy cards perhaps, and cling devotedly to familiar habits of worship and prayer. There is nothing new and exciting about these people. They are so ... predictable. Perhaps even "rigid".

Strangers, too, I say. Any Christian, as Saint Paul tells us, remains a "stranger". "But if some of the branches were broken off, and you, a wild olive shoot, were grafted in their place to share the richness of the olive tree ..." (Rom 11:17). Every gentile is a stranger, an alien branch grafted onto a tree where we had no business being in the first place.

The Lord has welcomed these strangers; in welcoming them, we welcome the Lord in return.

# 41

# Of Feasts and Families

I do not know a command of Jesus that seems to have been so universally disobeyed as the one we heard recently in a Sunday Gospel: "When you give a feast, invite the poor, the maimed, the lame, the blind" (Lk 14:13).

"Ah, but my parish does this on Thanksgiving Day; it holds a dinner for the homeless. We contribute canned goods." I'm sorry, but that is not what the Greek says precisely. Only the New American Standard Bible (the most literal of the common translations) gets it fully right: "whenever you give a banquet". Jesus is stating a general rule, not something you satisfy by doing once in a while. On each and every occasion on which you give a banquet, He says, this is what you are to do.

Furthermore, He implies that *only* those who lack the means to repay you (Lk 14:14) should be invited. To invite a token poor person or two would not come up to the intention of His command.

I have been to thousands of "banquets"—Luke's word (*doche*) covers any kind of reception or show of hospitality—open houses, "mixers", after-event receptions, cocktail hours, wedding receptions (of course), fundraising dinners, not to mention family gatherings and dinner parties. Not once, when Christians were hosting, was Our Lord's rule followed. A saying that should always be followed is never followed.

So what is going on here? Is the saying without application? Is it so hyperbolic that it is fundamentally impractical?

Oddly, an argument in Adam Smith's *Wealth of Nations* clarified the teaching for me. Where have all the feasts gone?—Smith asks at one point (III. iv). One can read in medieval and ancient histories, he says, that wealthy men hosted feasts on a near daily basis. The practice was common among Highland chieftains, Smith points out, even until the early 1700s.

I remember Sir Walter Scott's description of such a feast at the beginning of *Waverley*. In *Quo Vadis*, another example, the feasts at Caesar's court are a big temptation. Of course, John the Baptist was executed by a licentious Herod at one of his feasts. But in modern societies, the practice has lapsed. Leave it to Adam Smith to wonder why.

"In a country which has neither foreign commerce," Smith explains, "nor any of the finer manufactures, a great proprietor, having nothing for which he can exchange the greater part of the produce of his lands which is over and above the maintenance of the cultivators, consumes the whole in rustic hospitality at home. If this surplus produce is sufficient to maintain a hundred or a thousand men, he can make use of it in no other way than by maintaining a hundred or a thousand men."[1]

Thus wealthy men, "from the sovereign down to the smallest baron", have ever had their retinues of loyal supporters, with whom they feasted constantly. And any excess beyond this was used to foster greater dependency among the tenant farmers. This was how the wealthy kept

---

[1] Adam Smith, *The Wealth of Nations* (New York: P. Collier, 1902), bk. 3, chap. 4, p. 108.

their power, Smith says, by fostering dependence, mainly through feasts.

Smith is developing an argument of David Hume's that, curiously, the rise of manufacture and foreign trade led to the breakup of baronial power, since the wealthy could now spend their money on accumulating luxurious artifacts. In doing so, true enough, they still "supported" the network of manufacturers and traders who supplied these luxuries. But they had no power over this network, from its dispersion, and because their own contribution to its maintenance was relatively small. In this way the rise of commercial society supported the rise of a free society.

I am not interested here in evaluating this fascinating argument. Clearly, what Smith regards as freedom, the autonomy of consumers and producers, has downsides that we have grown increasingly worried about. Also, analogues of the medieval lord and his dependent retinue are alive and well in contemporary wealth-transfer politics.

The point I wish to emphasize, rather, is that in traditional societies the "banquet" stands for the use of surplus wealth. Our Lord is engaging in what rhetoricians call the synecdoche of *pars pro toto*—he refers to one use of surplus wealth, the only available use at the time, to refer vividly to any use of surplus wealth.

The command about banquets, then, is a command to use surplus wealth for almsgiving. Of course it retains its validity in commercial societies.

And yet some Christians have satisfied the command in close to its original meaning. Saint Elizabeth of Hungary and Saint Margaret of Scotland come to mind. These women essentially swapped out the retinues of their royal courts, replacing them with the poorest of the poor. Instead of feasting hundreds of noblemen and sycophants on a daily basis, these saints were famous for setting up hospitals near their palaces and taking care of the crippled, the lame, and the blind before anyone else.

But the other Christians who do so are parents, especially parents of large families. I mention large families because the total commitment of surplus wealth is usually clearer in that case, and the dinner tables of large families look the most like the outlay of a medieval court.

Their children are blind, that is, uneducated; certainly poor, without any legal title to possession; crippled— some cannot even walk—and lame, that is, immature. They cannot repay now, and, if they are raised well, they will not repay, since the best way they can show gratitude is by doing the same for their own children later.

We must reject the false arguments that parents who generously welcome children are only selfishly "actualizing" themselves or that, as they have helped cause their own children to exist, there is no merit in their caring for them. Certainly, such parents serve the common good by having many children in a time of catastrophic demographic decline.

Yes, parents of large families faithfully keep this commandment of Our Lord with great clarity.

Part V

# Life and Manners

## 42

# The Merely Human Condition

"Into this world we're thrown / Like a dog without a bone." So sang Jim Morrison of The Doors. (Imagine those words of course with the tune from "Riders on the Storm".) Apparently, Morrison once heard a lecture on the German philosopher, Martin Heidegger, where the speaker was explaining the existentialist notion that we exist as if "thrown into" this world (in German, *Geworfenheit*, "thrown-ness"). Such a concept is, of course, particularly appealing to alienated teenagers. Children after a divorce or in current government schools understandably feel as if they are simply tossed, uncaringly, into their milieu.

In this triad—The Doors, Martin Heidegger, American teenagers—we see that there is a battle for construing who we are, where we came from, and where we are going. The battle is decided at a level almost too deep for words. What is Christianity's position in this battle? Does it agree we are thrown into the world like a dog without a bone? If not, what does it say? "The world" takes Christianity to be superficial and silly, telling a tale like "things were good in the past, and our work is to make them good again." And perhaps some Christians even believe that.

But if we look more carefully, we see that Christianity begins with something even darker than "thrown-ness", and things get even worse from there, so to speak.

Christianity does not merely hold that we are thrown into the world like a dog without a bone. It is more like we are thrown into the world like a puppy, with a predator lurking in the shadows, looking for the moment to destroy it. Everything young and new and fragile is particularly at risk.

At least this is what I have learned from Sacred Scripture, when I study it with the interpretive key that "only in the mystery of the incarnate Word does the mystery of man take on light" (*Gaudium et Spes*, no. 22). The baby Christ is born, and Herod wipes out a generation of children to destroy Him. The Woman is about to give birth, and a great red dragon "stood before the woman who was about to bear a child, that he might devour her child when she brought it forth" (Rev 12:4).

How many families of ten or twelve children in past centuries saw only one live to adulthood? If disease is properly interpreted, in general, as a sign and result of sin, then the sin of mankind without doubt has attacked children primarily. And, as if it is a rule that cannot be escaped, the moment the human race conquered childhood infectious diseases, we started killing children of our own accord.

So this is the first truth: We are generated into a "world" that is set upon our destruction precisely when we are weakest and most vulnerable. In this context, Christian marriage appears as a stronghold and refuge.

But it gets darker. This "world" is set against truth as much as new life. So also, I have learned from Scripture: "The light shines in the darkness, and the darkness has not overcome it" (Jn 1:5). And yet it wanted to overcome it—this is the point. John the Baptist was eliminated for telling the truth (we remembered his Passion yesterday). And so were most of the prophets. Jesus lasted only one week in Jerusalem.

The principle is confirmed without fail. Even the unjust victors write the history. Governments govern by controlling how their subjects perceive things. We are dismayed that there is no longer any "reckoning" or "clearing" of truth by public authorities: think of Hunter Biden's laptop, the Russia collusion hoax, the lab origin of COVID-19. And yet this has always been the human condition. (Granted, a republic founded on a proposition was supposed to be the exception. But can it be?)

It gets darker still. In finding our way, we cannot follow "the many". We must somehow find and follow "the few", perhaps the very few. "You shall not follow a multitude to do evil" (Ex 23:2). "Enter by the narrow gate; for the gate is wide and the way is easy, that leads to destruction, and those who enter by it are many" (Mt 7:13). "This is no time for believing everyone; believe only those whom you see modelling their lives on the life of Christ" (Saint Teresa of Avila).[1]

Chesterton was wrong that tradition is the democracy of the dead; it is the aristocracy of the dead, where time has winnowed away everyone except the very few who are potentially worth following.

And then, darker still: if you take upon yourself the difficult task of following the few who are righteous, you most assuredly will be ridiculed, mocked, deserted, and attacked—and possibly betrayed or subverted.

And then, even darker: you will find that there is something within you that wants to undermine yourself and your best efforts, ready to turn whatever good you do, without your hardly being able to notice it, into something ghastly and even demonic. And so you must be constantly on guard against whatever this is within you.

---

[1] *The Way of Perfection*, trans. E. Allison Peers (New York: Image, 1964), chap. 21.

Yes, while you are trying your best to walk against the wind with the righteous, you must exercise extreme vigilance and constantly humble yourself, mortify yourself, strive for greater self-knowledge, and constantly convert, as if for the first time—or you will be lost. And then at the end of the day, you will find that your best efforts, although necessary, are not sufficient, and that certainly thinking, purpose, resolution, good intentions—all fail in the battle and count as if for naught. And it will be something simple, material, and fleshly, like holy water, a vocal prayer, or a priest's anointing, that will prove your salvation.

There is so much more to be said, but this is a start. It is certainly a step in the right direction to acknowledge that, unless we constantly turn to Christ, "Into this world we're thrown / Like a dog without a bone."

# 43

# Heresies of Presumption

There are certain goods Catholics enjoy that they can take for granted. This takes the form: they presume, usually on a false philosophy, that those goods are available to everyone, just as a basic fact, rather than solely as a consequence of the sacrifice of Our Lord. And then they get all mixed up about the uniqueness of Christianity or *extra ecclesiam nulla salus.*

Such persons are practical heretics, although they may not know it and do not mean to be. It is not that they deny a truth of the faith affirmed in the Creed. They do not say, for example, that there is only one person in God (Unitarianism) or that Jesus is not divine (Arianism). Rather, they suppose something false, practically speaking, about the way of salvation. I suspect many Catholics are like this because, raised in the faith, they do not know the faith. Converts are much less likely to go wrong by presumption.

Here is an example. I believe that I have direct access to the Most High God any time, simply by turning to Him. I may have offended Him many times already during the day. I may currently be distracted by something foolish rather than doing what I should. But I presuppose this: if I simply turn to Him, maybe to ask for help, as if He is waiting only to converse with me, no matter my faults, He will assuredly hear my prayer.

If someone asked why I presume this, I would appeal to my divine sonship, my "Divine Filiation", as spiritual writers call it. I would say: "Jesus as the only-begotten Son had this sort of relationship with the Father. By Baptism, I am made a son of God also and enjoy a similar relationship. Does not the Our Father, said with a certain meaning by a Christian, express and confirm this fact?"

My life as a whole has a certain character because I live it in the awareness that conversing with God is as easy as turning to Him, which is within my power. If I stay free from mortal sin, I always live thus "in the presence of God", then, and it is up to me to seek to live this most fully by familiar means taught us by the saints—the crucifix, images, short ejaculatory prayers, "offering it up", regular times of mental prayer, seeking the sustenance of the Eucharist.

But my knowledge of philosophy, history, and other religions tells me two things. The first is that this is an extraordinary presumption, which has no rational basis in the nature of things and which few outside of Christianity have supposed. I cannot even speak with the president when I wish, at my convenience. Certainly, a constant propensity to side with his opponents would make that prospect even more unlikely. I do not have the billions of dollars necessary to get to the edge of space through my efforts—how to ascend, then, through the levels of the Great Chain of Being to arrive at the Heavenly Court? I am a mortal, just dust. Why should the gods even know about me, and, if they do, why would they care?

"So you can just turn to God—the true God, the Creator and Father of all, from all eternity—whenever you wish, and gain His ear and even His favor just by wishing it? On what basis exactly? How did you acquire such powers?" A Christian has an answer, which is genuine, reliable, and true, but does anyone else? "But to all who received him, who believed in his name, he gave power to become children of God; who were born, not of blood nor of the will of the flesh nor of the will of man, but of God" (Jn 1:12–13).

This is the first thing I see from my studies, that the presumption is extraordinary and rare outside of Christianity because it has no basis in our nature, viewed with sobriety.

The second thing is that, nonetheless, false philosophies have promised or implied something similar. Most obvious would be those who say that God is within each of us, or a fragment of God, or maybe even that, simply by being created, we are identical with God or united with Him. Descartes, for instance (to take one of the less egregious cases), seemed to have believed that the very essence of God was represented in the human soul and that we need do no more than peer within to see that, by necessity, He exists. For Descartes, this is what *imago Dei* meant. More recent philosophies of radical autonomy seem to suppose implicitly that we are gods.

In a Christian or post-Christian society, we might still say about these false approaches to familiarity with God what Saint Thomas Aquinas said about the famous "Ontological Argument" of Saint Anselm: "[Such an] opinion arises from the custom by which from their earliest days people are brought up to hear and to call upon the name of God. Custom, and especially custom in a child, comes to have the force of nature. As a result, what the mind is steeped in from childhood it clings to very firmly, as something known naturally and self-evidently."[1]

Premises must be self-evident; cultural inheritance easily looks like an unquestioned premise. Yes, our culture is very much post-Christian. But trace back its popular

[1] Thomas Aquinas, *On the Truth of the Catholic Faith: Summa contra Gentiles*, trans. Anton C. Pegis (New York: Image Books, 1955), bk. 1, chap. 11, no. 1.

presumptions about chumminess with God and its philosophical assumptions of "autonomy"—trace them back
really, causally and historically—and you will be pointed
to Baptism and the condition articulated by John, "but as
many as received him". *Extra ecclesia nulla salus.*

But it is not only direct access to God that we presume to
exist without Christianity, but also eternal life that is blessed
and full; fellowship with all human beings that is familial;
confidence and hope in some kind of progress in history;
the enchantment of daily life; and the eternal significance
of beauty.

All these, viewed truthfully, are from the active power
of Christianity—alone.

# 44

# On Politeness and Brutalism

"Whoever says '*raka!*' to his brother shall be liable to the council. And whoever says, 'You fool!' shall be liable to the Gehenna of fire" (Mt 5:21–22; AT).

It is possible to set down a continuum of vices and virtues in the stance we take toward others. On one end, there is brutalism, which encompasses murder. On the other end, there is politeness. In between, there are increasing grades of perfection, a.k.a. virtues. Politeness, from the Latin root word for polish, is the extreme of perfection. We laugh at "polishing schools", but the fundamental idea is sound. And our society would be much better if our colleges were polishing schools, too, instead of animal houses.

The grades are not unlike construction. A builder first "roughs out" his product. Then he completes it. Then he adds "finishing touches". Last of all, he polishes it. Try to polish a roughed-out bathroom, and you will understand how someone intent on polishing himself must first accomplish the steps in between.

Minimally one refrains from harm in speech and from needlessly causing pain. Call this "kindness". If you have nothing good to say, then say nothing at all. Hold your tongue. Bite your tongue. Stay calm and carry on.

The plethora of proverbs and sayings on this point shows how widespread this basic grade of perfection can be—and once was. It is a trait obviously related to discretion and circumspection, which extends out to these. It requires a minimal interiority and self-command—a self-conscious gap between what one would spontaneously say and, as if playing a role, what one does say.

Probably every virtue has a counterfeit, just as flattery is counterfeit love. In our day, a sentimental affirmation of every opinion of everyone passes for this kindness. But since it is relativism, it provides no rational guidance for action—and can coexist with a deep-seated brutalism.

The next stage of perfection can be called "refinement". Here one does not merely refrain from causing harm and pain, but one actually steers others in a better direction, helping others and bringing them pleasure, but without its being apparent that that is happening. For example, you express a wish in the right circumstances—which serves as the only command you give. Or a humorous remark, springing from genuine goodwill, has the effect of correcting, without giving offense.

With refinement, we already see a complication of language. Together with a refinement of character is a refinement of language and of self-knowledge. To give a simple example, "Pick up those boxes!" requires no more than the imperative mood. But "I have been thinking how great this room would look if those boxes were put in place" requires a hypothesis, the subjunctive mood, and imaginative indirection.

Politeness to some extent is just greater refinement. But politeness especially shows itself in a reciprocal exchange, when your interlocutor is equally refined, and each takes pleasure in the other's creative response to his refinement. It is as if, in tennis, kindness is simply keeping the ball in play; refinement is hitting good shots; and politeness is matching your opponent's skill with one's own worthy, corresponding skill, to keep a rally going. In politeness the social excellence of the other gets answered, not just his circumstances or actions.

In *The Count of Monte Cristo* by Dumas, an arrogant and cold-hearted magistrate (Villefort) at one point visits the Count, merely out of a sense of duty, to thank him for having saved his son's life. "The notable service that you performed yesterday for my wife and son", he says, "has put me under an obligation to thank you. I have therefore come to accomplish this duty and to express my gratitude to you."[1]

That is polished speech, indeed, but it does not spring from a polished character. Villefort is "signaling" his own virtue (as we would say), which is indiscreet in the circumstances. Furthermore, he is attempting to place the Count in an inferior position.

The Count sees these things and defends his honor with the utmost politeness:

> Monsieur ... I am very happy at having been able to preserve a son for his mother, for they say that the feeling of maternal love is the holiest of all; and my enjoyment of this happiness released you, Monsieur, from the necessity of fulfilling a duty, the accomplishment of which undoubtedly flatters me, knowing as I do that M. de Villefort is not prodigal with the honor that he does me, but which, precious though it may be, is less valuable to me than my sense of inner satisfaction.[2]

Dumas writes that Villefort "was astonished by this unexpected sally and winced like a soldier feeling a

[1] Alexandre Dumas, *The Count of Monte Cristo*, trans. Robin Buss (New York: Penguin, 2003), chap. 48.
[2] Ibid.

sword-thrust beneath his armor."[3] One might spend a fair bit of time analyzing the Count's response. Note how he refers to the mother's love, not the father's. He refers to Villefort in the third person, which matches the other's viewpoint of mere legal obligation. He uses the phrase "knowing as I do" to advert to Villefort's reputation. He minimizes through exaggeration ("undoubtedly flatters me") and alludes to a philosophical theory (egoism—"less valuable than my sense of inner satisfaction").

The exchange also shows that politeness—unlike our dubious "civility"—cannot be expected to bear the weight of all the virtues. But it is one among several, with its proper use. Indeed, Dumas tells us that Villefort "did not henceforth consider Monte Cristo a very civil gentleman"![4] The evil Villefort was merely civil, as were his flatterers.

Recall that *Monte Cristo* was fabulously successful when it first came out, serialized. While I am reading *Monte Cristo* to my younger children this summer,[5] even the six-year-old listens on intently. Like the others, she finds this language fascinating. What would it be like to think in this way, to speak in this way? Can we aspire to politeness, to an extreme of virtue, in our conversation with others, as we do in sports or music?

[3] Ibid.
[4] Ibid.
[5] Published August 8, 2019.

# 45

# On Sacrifice

The *Wall Street Journal* ran a brief column last week[1] by Charlotte attorney Mike Kerrigan about how his Irish Catholic mom used to advise him about any disappointment: "Offer it up!" The *Journal* editors headlined the piece, "My Mom's Christian Lesson". But the fact that it was published at all, and (if my experience is any basis for judging) widely shared, shows that it spoke to something universal.

"There used to be a form of devotion—perhaps less practised today but quite widespread not long ago—that included the idea of 'offering up' the minor daily hardships that continually strike at us like irritating 'jabs', thereby giving them a meaning," Kerrigan wrote. "In this way, even the small inconveniences of daily life could acquire meaning and contribute to the economy of good and of human love. Maybe we should consider whether it might be judicious to revive this practice ourselves."

This is what Pope Benedict XVI taught in his encyclical *Spe Salvi*.[2]

Saint Thomas Aquinas, in his treatment of "sacrifice" in the *Summa*, gives an explanation for why this practice

[1] Published May 11, 2021.
[2] Pope Benedict XVI, Encyclical Letter *Spe Salvi*, on Christian Hope, November 30, 2007, no. 40.

remains appealing, even if it has become—for our current moment and practically speaking—defunct.

> The offering of sacrifice to God [he says] belongs to the law of nature: Natural reason tells man that he is subject to a higher being, on account of the defects which he perceives in himself, and in which he needs help and direction from someone above him: and whatever this superior being may be, it is known to all under the name of God. Now just as in natural things the lower are naturally subject to the higher, so too it is a dictate of natural reason in accordance with man's natural inclination that he should tender submission and honor, according to his mode, to that which is above man. Now the mode befitting to man is that he should employ sensible signs in order to signify anything, because he derives his knowledge from sensibles. Hence it is a dictate of natural reason that man should use certain sensibles, by offering them to God in sign of the subjection and honor due to Him, like those who make certain offerings to their lord in recognition of his authority. Now this is what we mean by a sacrifice, and consequently the offering of sacrifice is of the natural law.[3]

(Note: Astute Catholics might judge a theory of natural law as to whether it can immediately give a good account, like this, of a general and primary obligation to offer sacrifice to God. Whether the so-called "new natural law" can do so, for instance, is highly doubtful.)

We all feel this pull. We understand implicitly that our lives should be characterized by sacrifice and are missing something if they are not. Indeed, Newman makes it an argument for Catholicism, over and against Protestantism, that in the sacrifice of the Mass the Church best realizes

---

[3] *Summa Theologica* II-II, q. 85, a. 1, corpus.

the religious impulse that long pre-existed in paganism: "In all sacrifices it was specially required that the thing offered should be something rare, and unblemished; and in like manner in all atonements and all satisfactions, not only was the innocent taken for the guilty, but it was a point of special importance that the victim should be spotless, and the more manifest that spotlessness, the more efficacious was the sacrifice."[4]

Citing the great penitential psalm, "The sacrifice acceptable to God is a broken spirit" (51:17), Aquinas says outward sacrifices are meant to be signs of a more fundamental inward sacrifice, which he calls "reverence" or "the offering to God of a devout mind". Outward sacrifices, in the strict sense, consist in the giving up and destruction (for you) of something of value, which in your culture signifies worship. These are actions, Aquinas says, which would have no value and would not be done except to honor and display subjection to God: think of animal sacrifice. But the acts of the various virtues, too, which should, in any case, be done, can in an extended sense count as sacrifices, if they are done for the ultimate motive of glorifying God. This is where one would place "offer it up!" It is an exhortation to show courage, steadfastness, equanimity, patience, or humility, but as directed to God, in an attitude that we came from Him, and are returning to Him, and are not our own persons.

Virtues involving the use of the body especially show our "spiritual worship", as Saint Paul taught (Rom 12:1), and as the Apostles urged the early converts in insisting that they "abstain from fornication" (Acts 15:29; AT).

---

[4] See "Natural Religion", in *Grammar of Assent* (Notre Dame and London: Univ. of Notre Dame Press, 1986), bk. 2, chap. 10, no. 1, pp. 316–17.

If the natural law of sacrifice is universal, does it show itself inevitably, even insofar as people fall away from God?

I am inclined to say "yes and no". Let's first take the "no". When Bill and Melinda Gates announced their divorce last week, they used this language: "After a great deal of thought and a lot of work on our relationship, we have made the decision to end our marriage."

A Christian might read this and think, "If you really were married, then God joined you together, and therefore 'you' cannot decide to end it on your own." A simple, polytheistic pagan upon hearing this might have thought, "What does your god have to say about it?" Certainly, the notion that we all are in service to a higher god through the body seems to be lost when God is lost.

But the "yes" arises from the worry that, when a society dethrones the true God, it puts a multitude of gods in his place—namely, our autonomous selves, each of which claims the authority to define the mystery of the universe.

So I worry that the destruction of the innocents around us, especially in their bodies—seduction, corruption, abortion, mutilation—arises not from alleged necessity, bad jurisprudence, mere social injustice, or even false ideas of liberty, but from a dark service to false gods, which must have their victims and blood.

# 46

# Thanks within Thanks

Let us suppose that on Thanksgiving Day your mother, a woman of outstanding Catholic piety and adorned with the virtues, has baked an artisanal loaf of sourdough bread and, having sliced off a piece, has placed it still steaming, buttered, before you on a plate. Smiling, she awaits your response.

Something of the highest nobility has been done for you, and now it becomes a test, to see whether your character is appropriate to the gift.

According to Saint Thomas Aquinas (*ST* II-II, 106), to respond properly to this kindness, you must draw upon four distinct virtues—not one, but four. These virtues are as if "nested" because the "principles" or causes of the bread's being given to you are themselves nested.

The First Cause of your having received this bread is God, who made you and your mother, and her virtues, and the wheat and everything else—God who is still intimately concerned with them, knowing even the number of molecules in the slice (like the hairs on your head) and—let's not omit it—also its flavorfulness and crumb, and how it specially delights you. This original cause of good requires on your part the response of "due cult" (as Saint Thomas puts it). And so you say a blessing, perhaps the traditional "Hamotzi" ("who brings forth"), like the one Jesus would have said:

*Baruch atah Adonai Eloheinu ...*
   "Blessed are You Lord, our God, King of the Universe, who brings forth bread from the earth."


To respond properly to this gift here and now, of this particular piece of bread, it becomes due, to you, to worship God.

What you say in worship is indeed a "blessing". We call it "saying grace". Yet "grace" here means expressing that we take pleasure (Latin: *gratus*) in the gift and the giver.

Or we can call it giving a "thank"—the original term was singular, related to "think"—meaning that we think of, we tarry in thought upon, the gift and the giver with delight. But because, strictly, we are thus turning with "thanks" toward the one we recognize as our Creator, we are worshipping God, through the virtue of religion. So religion is the first of the four virtues that we must show.

But the cause or "principle" of your receiving the bread there is not merely God, your Creator, but also your mother, your co-creator—without whom you would not have been born, would not have survived to sit there, and would not have learned the word "bread", or good manners in eating it, or that you should smile, and chew twenty-one times (or whatever), and break the bread before taking a bite.

And likely it was your mother who taught you the words even to "say grace". And so yes, a machine might stuff bread down your throat. But that you are in a position to "take and eat" it as a human being is mainly the work of your mother and father. "Everything that is received is received in the manner of the recipient", and this manner—"good manners"—is given to you by that woman there.

Now, a specific type of reverence and indeed "worship" (in the old sense) is due to our parents as such. You know exactly what this is if your mom has passed away, because no one else can give you bread in the way that it was your mom who gave you bread. Saint Thomas calls the habit of showing such reverence "piety". So this is the second virtue you need to draw upon: piety, nested within religion.

And if, as is likely, your mother taught piety to you also, then "your giving thanks is itself her gift." But she is God's gift, and thus "Thank you, mom" is twice nested within "Thank you, God."

But then your mother, we are supposing, is adorned with grace and virtues. Suppose she were Saint Zélie Guérin Martin (the mother of Saint Thérèse of Lisieux) or Saint Wiktoria Ulma. But perhaps it is enough to say: she is a baptized wife and mother in the state of grace. Such a dignity is already not natural: it is literally out of this world.

Or simply ponder what any mother can claim by way of achievement: the dignity and merits of nights getting up with her children, of scrubbing floors and cleaning, of feeling cares and shedding tears, of shopping for you and the never-ending car rides—all those dignities we honor mothers for (we used to honor mothers for) on Mother's Day. She has them even when it is not Mother's Day.

If a king or ambassador—if a celebrity or an elite athlete— had brought you the bread, you would have been overcome with astonishment. "Jordan Peterson was in my house, and he thought to cut a slice of bread and bring it to me." But one greater than Jordan Peterson (for you) is here.

A distinct virtue is needed for recognizing such excellence and for seeing it as a secondary cause under God, and ordered within paternal and maternal authority—we need a third virtue for expressing thoughts of delight ("thanks") on that basis. The ancients called it *observantia*, "observance".

And then, fourth, there is the mere fact that someone or other did some good thing or other to you: acting as a benefactor, to whom you are a beneficiary, not of a random, but of a deliberate act of kindness. Now the due response, when you look at the gift simply under the aspect of a benefactor and benefit, becomes simply "giving thanks"— purely so, with nothing added. Thus (Saint Thomas says) the fourth requisite virtue is "gratitude"—nested within the other three.

This Thanksgiving, then, give thanks that you can give a fourfold thanks. At dinner, give thanks for the benefaction of your fellow man, grateful, too, for God's polity of bestowed excellence, while you honor your mother and father, and bless the God of all creation who brings forth bread, and turkey and gravy, from the earth.

# 47

# Piety for Things

If the opposite of greed is detachment, then greed takes some very strange forms, because detachment does.

Let's call detachment any ordered use of material goods, while greed is disordered, disproportionate use. Modern, mechanical images of society conceptualize greed as something like an excessive draw of energy—too much fuel demanded and expended by a part. Older, organic conceptions imagine it as disproportionate growth, grasping after more than is right for smaller parts such as yourself. On both of these simple images, the remedy for greed is something simple and a reduction: look for less, ask less, use less, consume less.

We can grant that greed is looking for "more" than you should (the Greek word is *pleonexia*, "more grasping"). But "more" can mean something other than quantity. Take C. S. Lewis' excellent lesson for Christians as regards gluttony. To be fastidious about food, caring about how it is prepared or spiced or heated or presented, beyond what is reasonable (sharp insistence on the perfect manner of each of these would be fully reasonable for the teacher in a cooking school), counts as gluttony, just as much as eating too many calories. Actually, wanting fewer calories can be gluttonous as well, say, when showing that you are unhappy about a food's richness would offend your host.

In my experience as a father, the original sin of children as regards anything conferred on them is abuse, not looking for more of that possession conceived of as stuff. But abuse is a kind of "more". The most recent instance (fresh from a week ago): my wife gave our youngest children inflatable dodgeballs for playing Four Square in our court over Thanksgiving. Despite repeated warnings against indoor play, such roughhousing was something they could not easily give up ... until the other day an errant throw hit a precious picture on the mantle, knocking it to the ground and breaking the glass.

This was, strictly, wanting more, *pleonexia*—wanting to use the balls in "more" places and "more" times than during daylight in the court. (For older children, as with Saint Augustine's youthful theft of pears, there might also be the "more" that is the thrill, simply, of deliberate lawlessness.)

Just as gluttony can be shown in "less", not more, quantity, so greed can be shown in "less" care about things, not more, especially when more care costs you something.

Our Lord wore a seamless garment, which He must have possessed since He had grown to full stature, perhaps twenty years, and yet which was still in such excellent condition that even rough soldiers did not want to damage it. After the feeding of the five thousand, Our Lord taught detachment (presumably) by insisting that the fragments be carefully gathered. From this verse alone we can infer that thrift is the opposite of greed.

In a famous homily, Saint Josemaria Escrivá comments:

> I preach that detachment is self-dominion. It is not a noisy and showy beggarliness, nor is it a mask for laziness and neglect. You should dress in accordance with the demands of your social standing, your family background, your work ... as your companions do, but to please God: eager

to present a genuine and attractive image of true Christian living. Do everything with naturalness, without being extravagant. I can assure you that in this matter it is better to err on the side of excess than to fall short.[1]

A rebuke against slovenly dress for church, to be sure, but also against every kind of lack of care that stems from ourselves and is not truly necessitated. The saint continues: "One of the signs that we're aware of being lords of the earth and God's faithful administrators is the care we take of the things we use: keeping them in good condition, making them last and getting the best out of them so that they serve their purpose for as long a time as possible and don't go to waste."

Of course, doing so is as difficult in the long run as clearing out a to-do list is in the short run.

Part of this detachment from things is attachment to the persons who made them. Our Lord was not a stoic who pretended He did not know where His seamless cloak came from when the soldiers rudely stripped Him of it. By His attachment to its maker, He made Himself all the more vulnerable to getting hurt when despoiled of it.

Reflections such as these seem salutary at the start of the Christmas shopping and gift-giving seasons.[2] Advent conversion for us might include prayerful reflection on where all these manufactured things came from. The two great failings of our countrymen today, I believe, are division and distraction, which feed each other.

How much of our polarization comes from not appreciating how many people from former generations sacrificed

---

[1] Josemaria Escriva de Balaguer, "Detachment", in *Friends of God* (Manila: Sinag-Tala, 1989), p. 178.

[2] Published December 7, 2022.

their "chance" in life, to build up this economy and culture for us? Or take the smartphone that you may be using to read this essay. Most likely, it was made in a mega-factory in China, where upward of 300,000 people live, eat, and sleep, working overtime up to twelve hours a day, each doing the same repetitive task, say, screwing in just one screw, for a couple of thousand phones each day, with one day off per week to see spouse, children, or grandparents.

The mega-factory (as an Apple executive once told me) has analogies with a college campus: it offers good work in that poor province of China; the workers wish to work there for a year or two; and smartphones are great works of brilliant design.

Still, it is difficult to work in such conditions. And piety for things, which implies solidarity with others, will lead me to ask: As a "faithful administrator", am I getting the best possible use of this machine? Or am I distractedly grasping for "more" in all the wrong places?

And there's a good place to start.

# 48

# The Color of Dinosaurs

A sentence in Chateaubriand's *Genius of Christianity*, truly one of the masterworks of apologetics, caught my attention recently: "God might have created, and doubtless did create, the world with all the marks of antiquity and completeness which it now exhibits."[1]

He stated this in the course of arguing that, for all we know, the biblical account of the world's age, about eight thousand years, could be actually true. The difficulty posed by fossils and rock strata, he said, was easily dismissed and "has been solved a hundred times" on that principle. Understand that Chateaubriand's book almost single-handedly reversed the remaining anti-clericalism of the French Revolution. It inspired Victor Hugo and other great lights of the next generation to "become like Chateaubriand" and prepared the ground for the Catholic "intellectual renaissance" in France a few decades later.

But here he was adamantly affirming a "New Earth" hypothesis, which many in our generation regard as fringe lunacy. Worse, he supposed it was obviously true.

I thought about the principle of the matter. Which was "better" to create: something that begins entirely "new"

[1] Francois-René Chateaubriand, *The Genius of Christianity* (Baltimore: John Murphy & Co., 1884), p. 136.

and develops after it is created, or something that is created "old" already, with a past that is only implicit, not itself created? We have a bias toward the former, I think, but why? Solely from familiarity with Darwin?

Surely, we must concede that God has the *power* to create something that carries a history with it already. Moreover, it would not be deceptive for Him to do so. We concede that God might create a mature human being, as Adam was supposed to be. But a mature human being presupposes a conception, development, and childhood. These would have to be solely attributed, not actually preexisting, in the case of an Adam.

We concede that God might create fine wine, as at Cana, and yet without having created first its terroir, blending, and long maturation—all necessary to a fine wine. The wine at Cana was exquisite but not deceptive.

There was a debate in the Middle Ages over the indeterminacy, from a scientific standpoint, of whether the universe was created by God "in time". This indeterminacy arises most sharply given cyclical processes in nature. Take procreation, for example. In an Aristotelian universe, procreation is a repeatable process stretching forward indefinitely into the future. Procreation is how a species of animal, as a kind, can achieve immortality and imitate God, in the only way it can—so says Aristotle explicitly.

But an animal's existence stretches *back into the past indefinitely*, just as much on the same principle. If revelation then tells us that, no, this cycle began "in time" about eight thousand years ago—fine, we accept it as true—but then we must concede (so a medieval philosopher might put it) that the first created animals carried along with them an infinite, attributed past.

Artists have no difficulty in accepting a creation with an implicit past. Novels do not need to begin with the protagonist as a conceptus. In many clever novels, the past is deliberately set as a puzzle to the reader as much as to the characters, and part of the fun of reading it is trying to figure out precisely which past is correctly attributed. Such is any mystery novel, and such was Dorothy Sayers' view of creation.

Implicit and attributed pasts will surely be present in the New Creation. Martyrs will show marks of their martyrdom, the tradition holds, not simply martyrs whose bodies remain incorrupt.

On balance, I think we must hold that to create beings with an implicit past is actually better. It is more nuanced and cleverer. It assigns more good to the creature. It implies creatures with signification as well as being.

One somewhat dizzying thought is how close to the present time Chateaubriand's conjecture might be extended. Bertrand Russell used to claim that there was no way for someone to tell whether he had just begun to exist five minutes ago. Everything would look exactly the same.

This kind of argument has greater force if I am an isolated Cartesian conscience, and memory is subjective; also, if one thinks that a private universe might just unaccountably jump into existence without a cause.

But if we are speaking about genuine creation, the act of a person, and like Chateaubriand we take "a people" such as the Jewish nation to be the unit of remembrance and memory to involve an objective relationship to what is, then the line can be drawn no later than their collective memory. Evidently, too, *the nature of time* would need to be rethought, presumably along the lines of Book XI of Saint Augustine's *Confessions*.

One fascinating upshot of Chateaubriand's approach is that the nature of scientific explanation of the past is reconceived, and, by extension, all scientific theory. Science really does become the attempt at reconstructing the intention of God from whatever "signification" is implicit in Creation.

This reconstruction will have indeterminacy exactly where, by design of course, that signification does not allow any determinate inference. My teacher W. V. Quine used to deride counterfactuals because such indeterminacy could not be eliminated from them: "Take, for instance, the possible fat man in the doorway; and again, the possible bald man in the doorway. Are they the same possible man, or two possible men? How do we decide? How many possible men are there in that doorway? Are there more possible thin ones than fat ones?"

And so on. But one might raise similar objections about anything left unsaid or not implied by a novelist.

So, when a created object's past is attributed, whatever could be definitely inferred would count as "science", while much might remain indeterminate.

Chateaubriand's conjecture, although exhilarating, has the sad upshot that, if true, dinosaurs did not actually exist. Reconstructing them becomes a kind of game. And if the evidence does not allow an inference to their color, they had no determinate color, and every boy is free to imagine whatever color he wishes.

# 49

# Liberty, *Modulo*

Because Catholicism is incarnational, it strives to become inculturated in whatever culture it is found, like yeast and like salt.

If I lived in Scotland, I would fancy hill walking, eat haggis with gusto (at least I would try to), listen to a lot of jigs and reels, and play perhaps even more golf. Since I live in America, that land with a Statue of Liberty (not a Statue of the Common Good), I regard myself as bound to love liberty.

If I did not love liberty already: some of us hear "Give me liberty or give me death", and it rings deep and rings true. In any case, I believe a Catholic American, as an American, is duty-bound to love liberty, and, as a Catholic, he is obliged to discover its true meaning and show it.

Almost the first thing I would want to say about liberty is that it is a glorious human good, to be desired as an end, not simply as a means.

I would quote Scripture in my defense: "Creation itself will be set free from its bondage to decay and obtain the glorious liberty of the children of God", says Saint Paul (Rom 8:21). He is speaking about the consummation, not the journey.

I would quote Saint Augustine: "God created us without us: but he did not will to save us without us,"[1] that is, without our consent. Therefore, to be saved is to be saved in freedom. I would refer to the teaching of Saint Thomas that the whole of life in Christ is charity, but charity is friendship with God, and there cannot be friendship without freedom. Friendship may be defined as the freest form of human relationship.

I would quote Cardinal Ratzinger, writing about theologies of liberation: "The Gospel of Jesus Christ is a message of freedom and a force for liberation."[2]

I would agree with Pope John Paul II who said in a homily at a Mass in Camden Yards, approvingly, that "America has always wanted to be a land of the free."[3]

That liberty is a good: this is a given. What liberty means: this is to be worked out. If "liberalism" is a commitment to liberty as a great human good, in cultural, social, economic, and political spheres, then count me as a liberal. And put me on record as saying that American Catholics need to be liberals, too.

I do not say such things on my own authority. The Gospel of Jesus Christ, as a force for liberation, "as a logical consequence", wrote Cardinal Ratzinger (in the same instruction quoted earlier), "calls for freedom from many different kinds of slavery in the cultural, economic, social,

[1] See *CCC*, no. 1847, which references St. Augustine, *Sermo* 169, 11, 13: *Patrologia Latina* 38, 923.

[2] Congregation for the Doctrine of the Faith, Instruction on Certain Aspects of the "Theology of Liberation" (August 6, 1984), http://www.vatican.va/roman_curia/congregation/cfaith/documents/rc_con_cfaith_doc_19840806_theology-liberation_en.html.

[3] John Paul II, Homily at Oriole Park, Baltimore (October 8, 1995), no. 6, https://www.vatican.va/content/john-paul-ii/en/homilies/1995/documents/hf_jp-ii_hom_19951008_baltimore.html.

and political spheres, all of which derive ultimately from sin, and so often prevent people from living in a manner befitting their dignity."

But I say freedom or liberty "modulo", as the mathematicians say, meaning "after one has made the necessary corrections or adjustments for something". This is a better way of speaking, in my view, than saying that we should desire liberty solely "as a means", to be exercised for the right end. It is better to say: we desire liberty as an end, but modulo three adjustments, which the Church has always insisted upon. I shall tell you what these are.

Before I do, I should say that freedom in Catholic thought is understood as a thing's operation in expression of the sort of thing it is, rather than its being acted upon from without against its nature.

As Pope Leo XIII explains in *Libertas*, his encyclical on freedom, what this means for a rational being is that true freedom is the expression of reason in our actions and emotions, and at the same time, it is a freedom from being directed by what is contrary to reason. Thus, both of what are called "positive" and "negative" freedom are contained in the Catholic conception. Now here are the three adjustments. The first is that the most fundamental freedom for us is freedom from sin. All other freedoms ultimately depend on this. Indeed, the main problem in "theologies of liberation", Ratzinger taught, was that they spoke as if unjust social structures were the fundamental unfreedom, rather than sin.[4]

The second adjustment follows from this. The mistaken "theologies of liberation" were based upon Marxist falsehoods about human nature. Freedom, however, essentially

---

[4] Congregation for the Doctrine of the Faith, "*Theology of Liberation*".

depends on truth. "The truth will make you free" (Jn 8:32). "The complete truth about man is the basis for any real liberation", Cardinal Ratzinger insisted.[5]

"Catholics of America!" Saint John Paul II concluded his homily, "Always be guided by the truth—by the truth about God who created and redeemed us, and by the truth about the human person, made in the image and likeness of God and destined for a glorious fulfillment in the Kingdom to come. Always be convincing witnesses to the truth."[6] (Remember that the word martyr means "witness".) No words could be more relevant today.

The third adjustment, in turn, follows upon this. Sin and dullness to truth are, as it were, the two great external impediments to freedom. But the internal one is a lack of virtue. To succeed in expressing our rationality in our actions and affections, we need to acquire the virtues, which implies following the natural law.

The old inscriptions on law schools said such things as "true freedom is obedience to law." Pope Leo teaches the same thing. For freedom to exist, "there must be law; that is, a fixed rule of teaching what is to be done and what is to be left undone.... In the moral necessity of our voluntary acts being in accordance with reason, lies the very root of the necessity of law."[7]

Thus, give me liberty or give me death!—but liberty modulo sin, ignorance, and lack of virtue.

[5] Ibid., no. 4.
[6] John Paul II, Homily at Camden Yards, no. 9.
[7] Leo XIII, encyclical letter *Libertas* (June 20, 1888), no. 7, https://www.vatican.va/content/leo-xiii/en/encyclicals/documents/hf_l-xiii_enc_20061888_libertas.html.

50

# Out of the Catholic Ghetto

Let us resolve to banish the phrase "Catholic ghetto" from our language forever. Or, if we do use it, let us use it precisely in the sense of Father John Tracy Ellis.

Arguably, "Ghetto" should never have been turned into a metaphor at all. It began in the sixteenth century as the proper name of the district in Venice where Jewish people were forced to live, walled off and under the watch of armed guards. For three hundred years it was only applied, by extension, to similar Jewish districts in European cities. In the twentieth century, the Nazis created new ghettoes during their short-lived Reich. How appropriate, then, if the name had remained forever affixed to such censurable practices, discarded once the Jewish Ghetto was abolished! "Ghetto" then might have joined "Pogrom" and "Race Law" in a linguistic museum of anti-Semitism.

Or, we might say, if it were allowed a metaphorical use, the Jewish people should have possessed it by right. Well, in fact, the first metaphorical use of the term was in an 1892 bestseller by Israel Zangwill, *Children of the Ghetto*, about the immigrant Jewish community of London. These people were not forced by law into anything. Rather, the ghetto in which they lived, Zangwill says, was "of voluntary formation":

People who have been living in a Ghetto for a couple of
centuries, are not able to step outside merely because the
gates are thrown down, nor to efface the brands on their
souls by putting off the yellow badges. The isolation im-
posed from without will have come to seem the law of
their being.[1]

Catholic immigrants to the United States in the nineteenth
century were not children of any ghetto. Admittedly they
sometimes faced Know Nothing hostility and the contempt
of successful Protestants. But they lived together in poorer
Italian, Irish, or French-Canadian neighborhoods because
when they arrived that was all they could afford. They
spoke little English, or spoke it poorly, and wanted to be
able to communicate easily with their neighbors. And they
could get on their feet more quickly if they lived alongside
relatives and friends from the old country. It would have
smacked of over-wrought self-pity if they had called their
neighborhoods "ghettoes", and it seems that they never did.

Rather, the phrase "Catholic ghetto" became common
much later, in the 1950s. For the phrase to appear to have
any sense at all, two further steps were necessary. First, it
became common to call African-American neighborhoods
"ghettoes". This was a reasonable enough metaphor, given
historic segregation and prejudice. Yet there was an unfortunate upshot: because the broad metaphorical meaning
depends on Zangwill's idea that a ghetto is "of voluntary
formation", to call a slum a "ghetto" is to imply as well
that those within are responsible for staying there.

Next, American Catholic intellectuals began to call
Catholic universities "ghettoes" by associating them with
the old immigrant neighborhoods. They did this in better

[1] Israel Zangwill, *Children of the Ghetto: A Study of a Peculiar People* (Cambridge: Black Apollo Press, 2011), p. 14.

and worse ways. Perhaps the best was a seminal essay in 1955 by Father John Tracy Ellis, "American Catholics and the Intellectual Life".[2]

American Catholics, he says, "have suffered from the timidity that characterizes minority groups, from the effects of a ghetto they have themselves fostered and, too, from a sense of inferiority induced by their consciousness of the inadequacy of Catholic scholarship." Anti-Catholicism is real, but it is not to blame: "The chief blame, I firmly believe, lies with Catholics themselves. It lies in their frequently self-imposed ghetto mentality, which prevents them from mingling as they should with their non-Catholic colleagues, and in their lack of industry and the habits of work."[3]

The notorious Land O' Lakes Agreement has received much attention, but Ellis' seminal essay, which set off a famous debate on "the state of Catholic intellectual life", deserves the greater attention if we believe that something went wrong and we want to diagnose why.

Ellis traces the "ghetto mentality" back to the Church's necessary concern with immigrants: "We do not need to be told what the immigrant status implied by way of poverty, hardship, yes, and even illiteracy.... We can easily understand how impossible it was for our ancestors to produce anything approaching a thriving intellectual life." There is an undeniable elitism in Ellis' essay. Nonetheless, he seems to write about these immigrants in the manner of an historian. Catholic colleges and universities, as a matter of fact, were founded originally to serve these groups. Hence, again, as a matter of fact, they likewise developed a mentality of separation.

We might think that Ellis' solution would be for Catholics—universities as well as individuals—to reject

[2] *Thought: Fordham University Quarterly* 30, no. 3 (1955): pp. 351–88.
[3] Ibid., p. 380.

their immigrant subcultures and assimilate into mainstream American culture. Yet he clearly does not mean this.

In some central paragraphs, this becomes clear, where he charges Catholic universities with "a betrayal of that which is peculiarly their own":

> Woefully, lacking in the endowment, training, and equipment to make them successful competitors of the secular universities . . . the subjects in which they could, and should, make a unique contribution were sorely neglected.[4]

Ellis says that Catholic institutions have instead been "engrossed in their mad pursuit of every passing fancy that crossed the American educational scene, and [have] found relatively little time for distinguished contributions to scholastic philosophy." He approvingly cites the great president of the University of Chicago, Robert Maynard Hutchins, who reproached Catholic universities for not taking advantage of their claim to "the longest intellectual tradition of any institution in the contemporary world".[5]

So here is the important idea from Ellis. If we use the phrase "Catholic ghetto" at all, we should use it for simply, and nothing other than, the free choice of Catholics to remain separate from non-Catholics—presumably, when doing so would be better for us and for them. "To leave the Catholic ghetto" does not mean an imperative to assimilate or imitate. Most importantly, it cannot involve a betrayal of "what is distinctively our own", but must imply a greater attention to cultivating it.

[4] Ibid., p. 374.
[5] Ibid.

# ACKNOWLEDGMENTS

I wish to acknowledge here the unfailing support I have received from my editors, Bob Royal at *The Catholic Thing* and Greg Tracy at the *Boston Pilot*. Also, when I began planning this book, Brad Kelley, Eric Mader, and Paul Swope helped me to identify my best essays, and their encouragement since has been deeply welcome.